Popular Judaica Library
General Editor: Raphael Posner

MINOR AND MODERN FESTIVALS

Edited by Priscilla Fishman

KETER BOOKS
Jerusalem

110826

KETER BOOKS is an imprint of
ISRAEL PROGRAM FOR SCIENTIFIC TRANSLATIONS LTD.
P.O. Box 7145, Jerusalem

Cat. No. 25096
ISBN 0 7065 1386 x

Printed in Israel

CONTENTS

Unlike the High Holy Days and the three Pilgrim Festivals of Passover, Shavuot and Sukkot, the minor festivals of the Jewish calendar are less sacred institutions than they are popular celebrations of events important in the history of the Jewish people. They mark the various experiences of the Jews as a group, and respond to the emotional needs that emerged from these experiences.

Of all the festivals dealt with in this book, only *Rosh Ḥodesh,* the New Month, is mentioned in the Five Books of Moses, where it is listed alongside the Sabbath and festivals. The Purim celebration derives from the story related in the Book of Esther, while Ḥanukkah commemorates historic events that occurred in the Hasmonean period. Tu be-Av and Tu bi-Shevat, days of secular, non-Jewish origin, were given Jewish themes during the period of the Mishnah. The medieval period brought Lag ba-Omer into the Jewish calendar, and at the same time added new levels of meaning to other festivals that had long been celebrated. Finally, our own century has seen Israel Independence Day and associated commemorative days added to the calendar, to mark recent historic events of Jewish importance. After the chapter on *Rosh Ḥodesh,* the festivals are given in the order in which they appear in the Jewish year.

In the Jewish tradition a festival is generally characterized by three elements: (1) rejoicing, which mainly takes the form of ceremonial meals and abstention from work; (2) special prayers and synagogue rituals; and (3) ceremonies and customs adapted to the particular thematic concepts of the festivals. All these will be explored herein in detail.

Beyond the treasure-trove of factual information several general conclusions will emerge from reading this book. First, it will become apparent that while some minor festivals derive their standing from having been noted "officially" in the classical texts of Judaism, others have grown out of indigenous or borrowed folk customs. Taking strong hold in the imagination of the people, they were "Judaized", and eventually won a recognized and honored place in the Jewish calendar.

Secondly, it will be clear that despite minor differences in local customs or liturgy, all groups of Jews, no matter what their regional provenance or "ethnic" community affiliation, have jointly recognized the historic roots of the festivals, and have shared in the internalization of the Jewish concept or ideal that is unique to each day.

The third conclusion that emerges from this volume is that Judaism as a way of life has been responsive to the changing concerns of the Jewish people and has been able to provide ways to express new concepts of inspiration, comfort and meaning at different periods of history.

Among all the festivals of the Jewish year, *Rosh Hodesh,* the New Month (literally, "head of the month") is unique in that it is not celebrated once, but twelve times a year.

The Bible establishes *Rosh Hodesh,* the first day of each month, as a festival, listing it together with the Sabbath and other festivals, as a day to be marked with special observances. From references in various books of the Bible it is clear that it was a day of rest on which there was no trade, when people gathered in the sanctuary to serve God, when festive meals were held, and when visits were made to the prophet. However, nowhere in the Bible is work expressly forbidden on *Rosh Hodesh,* as it is on the Sabbath and festivals, and thus it is considered a "minor" festival.

1

The signs of the zodiac as depicted on a medal struck in honor of Israel's 25th anniversary.

Determining the New Month

The Jewish calendar is both lunar and solar. That is, the months are determined by the periodic appearance and disappearance of the moon, while the seasons are fixed by the position of the sun in the sky. The festivals are dependent on both the month and the season.

The Months of the Year

The Jewish year consists of twelve months of 29 or 30 days, and totals 353 or 354 days. Because the solar year exceeds it by 11 days, an adjustment, or "intercalation" must be made. This is accomplished by adding a thirteenth month in certain leap years (see page 4).

The months of the year are:

Nisan (March—April)	Tishrei (September—October)
Iyyar (April—May)	Ḥeshvan (October—November)
Sivan (May—June)	Kislev (November—December)
Tammuz (June—July)	Tevet (December—January)
Av (July—August)	Shevat (January—February)
Elul (August—September)	Adar (February—March)

The month of Adar Sheni (second Adar) is added in leap years.

Sanctification of the Moon

In ancient times, the calendar was determined by direct observation of the moon. On the thirtieth of each month, the members of the Sanhedrin (Great Court) would assemble in a courtyard in Jerusalem and wait for two reliable witnesses to come and testify that they had personally observed the reappearance of the crescent moon in the sky.

Even at a later date, when astronomical calculations were used to ascertain the date of the new moon, *Rosh Ḥodesh* could still be proclaimed only on the testimony of witnesses whose evidence was, however, checked by astronomical calculations.

After the witnesses were examined, and the rabbis were satisfied with the report, the Sanhedrin would solemnly sanctify that day as *Rosh Ḥodesh*. If the crescent was observed on the twenty-ninth or thirtieth of the month, the thirtieth day was *Rosh Ḥodesh*. If no witnesses saw the moon's crescent even on the thirtieth day of the month, the following day was automatically sanctified as *Rosh Ḥodesh*.

As soon as the Sanhedrin had proclaimed the New Month, *Communicat-* steps were taken to inform the scattered Jewish communities of *ing the News* that fact. Beacons were lit atop the Mount of Olives; upon seeing this signal, bonfires would be lit on nearby hills, and in turn on more distant hills, until the news even reached communities outside the Land of Israel.

At a somewhat later period, the Samaritans (a sect which had broken away from the main body of the Israelites and developed its own religious practices) sought to interfere with these lines of communication. They would light bonfires on hilltops on days that were not proclaimed as *Rosh Ḥodesh* by the Sanhedrin in order to confuse the distant communities.

When this procedure could no longer be relied upon, the Sanhedrin began to send messengers to the various Jewish communities. Because of the time it took for the messengers to reach the distant lands of the Diaspora and proclaim the New Moon, Jews in those communities always celebrated *Rosh Ḥodesh* on the thirtieth day of the month. On those occasions, when they were informed of its postponement to the thirty-first day, they observed this as a second day of *Rosh Ḥodesh*. Moreover, it was also decreed that outside the Land of Israel the festivals were to be observed for two days instead of one, lest the notification of the exact date be delayed. The added day was called "the second holiday of the Diaspora", and is observed in all communities outside the Land of Israel, with the exception of Reform congregations. Yom Kippur, however, was not extended to a second day, because of the hardship of fasting.

According to tradition, the practice of depending on eye- *The Fixed* witnesses to the appearance of the new moon was abandoned in *Calendar* the middle of the fourth century, when Hillel II established a

3

fixed calendar. While Hillel undoubtedly had a share in this important development, modern scholars tend to think that some elements in the Jewish calendar predate Hillel, while others may have been introduced much later.

The calendar established rules for ascertaining when the new moon would appear without having to rely on direct observation, and for adapting the lunar year to the longer solar year. This was important, in order to ensure that the festivals which were celebrated on specific dates in the months would also fall in the appropriate agricultural seasons of the year. Without any adjustment, the festivals would "wander," and the spring festival of Passover, for example, would eventually fall in winter.

The required adjustment to the solar year is made by adding an extra month, Adar Sheni, in seven out of each cycle of 19 years. (Nineteen solar years of 365 days exceed 19 lunar years by about 209 days, which are approximately seven lunar months). Before the calendar was fixed, this adjustment had been made, in individual years, according to observed agricultural conditions, since the position of the sun determines the rate of growth of the crops. Hillel's calendar established that the extra month of Adar Sheni was to be added to the third, sixth, eighth, eleventh, fourteenth, seventeenth and nineteenth years of the cycle.

The "secret of calendar intercalation" was jealously guarded from outsiders — both Jewish and non-Jewish — by those who knew it, for the fixing of the calendar was an expression of authority over the entire Jewish people.

The Sabbath of Blessing
By astronomical calculation, the beginning of the month takes place at the moment when the moon's position is exactly between the earth and the sun, and it cannot be seen. That moment is known, in Jewish calendrical terminology, as the *molad,* the "birth" of the moon. Some six hours later, a fraction of the moon becomes visible, and the new month can be pro-

4

claimed. With the aid of the fixed calendar and precise astronomical calculations, the moment of the *molad* can be determined well in advance. Since the 8th century, it has been

The *Yehi Razon*
prayer recited on
the Sabbath preceding
Rosh Hodesh, from the
Harrison Miscellany,
Italy, 18th century.

customary in Jewish communities throughout the world, to announce the date of the forthcoming *Rosh Ḥodesh* on the Sabbath preceding it. This is known as *Shabbat Mevarekhin*, the "Sabbath of Blessing". (In Yiddish it is known as the *Shabbes* of *Rosh Ḥodesh bentshn*.) The month of Tishrei is not blessed in advance, since it is also Rosh ha-Shanah, and everyone knows when it will occur.

5

Following the reading of the portion from the Prophets on *Shabbat Mevarekhin,* the reader leads the congregation in announcing and blessing the coming month. It is customary to stand during this ceremony in remembrance of the practice of the Sanhedrin in Jerusalem, which stood while proclaiming the New Month.

In the Ashkenazi rite, a special prayer is recited for the House of Israel which begins: "He who wrought miracles for our fathers and redeemed them from slavery unto freedom, may He speedily redeem us and gather our exiles from the four corners of the earth, even all Israel united in fellowship, and let us say Amen." Many Sephardi and Oriental rites also include prayers for the well-being of the rabbis.

The reader takes the Torah scroll, announces the exact time of the *molad,* and proclaims the day(s) of the week on which *Rosh Ḥodesh* is to be celebrated. The ceremony concludes with a prayer that the New Month be for life, peace, gladness, salvation, and consolation for the House of Israel. After each phrase of this prayer is read aloud by the reader, the congregation responds, *"Amen, ken yehi raẓon* ('may it be Thy will')."

Yom Kippur Katan

In the second half of the 16th century a custom arose among the kabbalists (mystics) of Safed to observe the eve of the New Month as a day of fasting and repentance. They called the day *Yom Kippur Katan,* the "Minor Day of Atonement".

These mystics interpreted the waning of the moon as a symbol of the exile of the *Shekhinah* (Divine Presence), and the shrinking of the power of holiness after the Jews were exiled from Jerusalem. The reappearance of the moon was seen as a symbol of the return to perfection in the future age of redemption.

Besides the reading of the Torah and of the prayers that are generally recited on a fast day, special *seliḥot* (penitential prayers) were written for the afternoon service on *Yom Kippur Katan.* They are based on the themes of exile and redemption.

Consecration of the Moon

In addition to proclaiming and blessing the New Month, some groups of Jews observe the ceremony of consecrating the new moon. The ceremony is known as *Birkat ha-Levanah* ("blessing of the moon"), or *Kiddush Levanah* ("sanctification of the moon").

During the biblical period, *Rosh Hodesh* undoubtedly was of much greater significance than it is now. Not only was the appearance of the new moon crucial for determining the calendar and proclaiming the religious festivals, but, the moon and the other heavenly bodies were considered to exert influence on human beings.

The peoples of the ancient Near East worshipped the moon, but the Torah warned the Israelites against participating in the moon cult, and convicted transgressors were punished by death. The moon cult was, nonetheless, introduced into Judah by King Manasseh, but was subsequently abolished by King Josiah.

In the time of the Jewish historian Josephus, belief in astrology appeared to be common among the Jews. Evidently, some of the talmudic sages also believed in the decisive role played by celestial bodies in determining human affairs.

Rabbinic literature designates the moon as "Jacob's luminary", while the sun symbolized Esau. The rabbis taught that the Jewish nation bases its calendar on the lunar year because they have a portion in this world and in the world-to-come, like the moon which can be seen both by day and by night. An eclipse of the moon is, therefore, considered an evil omen for Israel, and is attributed to four different sins: forgery, false testimony, breeding small cattle in Erez Israel (since they damage the crops of the field), and cutting down fruit trees (see page 69).

Blessing the moon in an 18th century Jewish
quarter in Germany.

Vestiges of early Jewish belief in astrology and the power of the moon remain in the common greeting, *mazal tov* ("good luck"), which literally means "good sign of the zodiac", and in the custom of some Jewish groups not to celebrate a marriage in the latter half of the month, while the moon is waning.

The blessing of the moon takes place at night, and only if the moon is clearly visible (not when it is hidden by clouds). Preferably it should be said in the open air. It can be recited from the third evening after the appearance of the new moon, until the fifteenth of the lunar month. After that day, the moon begins to wane.

Significance

According to the Talmud, "Whoever pronounces the benediction over the new moon in its due time welcomes, as it were, the presence of the *Shekhinah.*" The ceremony of *Kiddush Levanah* was considered by some sages to be of such significance that they believed that one who consecrated the new moon was assured of life during the entire month. The school of Rabbi Ishmael taught that had Israel merited no other privilege than to greet the presence of their Heavenly Father once a month by reciting the benediction over the new moon, it would suffice. Thus, it is recommended that the benediction be pronounced, if possible, on the evening following the Sabbath, when one is still in a festive mood and is dressed in one's Sabbath clothes. In the month of Av the ceremony should not be performed before the ninth, which is a fast day and in Tishrei it is performed at the termination of the Day of Atonement.

Prayers

In the Ashkenazi rite, the blessing of the moon is introduced by reciting Psalm 148:1—6; in the Sephardi rite Psalm 8:4—5 is added. Then God is praised as the Creator and Master of Nature, who renews the moon.

During the period of the Mishnah, the proclamation of the New Month by the Sanhedrin was celebrated with dancing and rejoicing. It is still customary to rise on the tips of the toes in the direction of the moon while reciting three times, "As I dance

9

The *Hallel* prayer from a late 14th century illuminated *Haggadah*.

toward thee, but cannot touch thee, so shall none of my evil-inclined enemies be able to touch me."

Among the biblical verses and talmudic quotations that make up the remainder of the ceremony of blessing the new moon, two phrases are of historic interest. They are "David, King of Israel, lives and endures" (which is repeated three times), and, "Peace be with you" *(Shalom aleikhem)* — to which the response is, "To you be peace" *(Aleikhem shalom)*.

The inclusion of these phrases in the blessing of the moon is a reminder of events that occurred during the period of Judah

10

ha-Nasi, the patriarch of Judea and the compiler of the Mishnah, who lived in the latter half of the second and the beginning of the third centuries.

Customarily, the Sanhedrin sat in Judea — first in Jerusalem, and then, after the destruction of the Temple, in Yavneh. The Sanhedrin retained as many of its prerogatives as the Roman authorities would permit it, and the rabbis who were its members sought to rebuild Jewish life, even though the spiritual center of that life had been destroyed. Thus, the Sanhedrin continued to proclaim the New Moon and to intercalate the year, in an effort to preserve the unity of the scattered Jewish people by providing a uniform calendar for the Land of Israel, and the communities in the Diaspora. (At one point an attempt was made to intercalate the year in Babylonia, but it resulted in confusion and divisiveness, and the rabbis in Israel insisted that the prerogative of making calendrical decisions be reserved for them alone.)

In the days of Judah ha-Nasi, the site of the Sanhedrin was transferred from Judea to Galilee. This was a period of Roman persecutions of the Jews, when the Rabbinical Court was denied authority to proclaim the New Month. The Talmud records that Judah ha-Nasi sent one of his disciples, Rabbi Ḥiyya, to a place called Ein Tov, to hear the testimony of witnesses who came, in secret, to report the appearance of the new moon, so that the proclamation of *Rosh Ḥodesh* could be made, and the information passed on.

In order to protect themselves against possible traitors, the rabbis decided upon a password — the phrase *David melekh yisrael ḥai ve-kayam*, "David, King of Israel, lives and endures." Undoubtedly this phrase was chosen because it voiced Israel's continuous hope for redemption by the Messiah, a descendant of King David, as well as their faith that the House of David would survive its persecutors and be rebuilt.

David, Lives and Endures

Only witnesses who were able to give this password were admitted to the Rabbinical Court. There they were greeted with

11

the words *Shalom aleikhem,* to which the witnesses replied, *Aleikhem shalom.*

Customs and Prayers

When the Temple stood, an additional sacrifice was offered after the regular morning sacrifice on *Rosh Ḥodesh,* the Sabbath and festivals. Simultaneous with the practice of offering a sacrifice, an additional prayer was also said on those days. Since the destruction of the Temple, and the cessation of the sacrifices, prayers have formally taken the place of the offerings.

    Temple Sacrifice

    Although work is permitted on *Rosh Ḥodesh,* it was the custom of Jewish women to refrain from certain work on that day. They would not undertake difficult labor such as weaving but would do light tasks, such as sewing. The rabbis did not object to this practice, and even sought to find a reason why women observe this day as a semi-holiday. They suggested that it was a reward for them, since the women did not surrender their jewelry in order to make the Golden Calf in the wilderness.

    Talmudic Practices

    On *Rosh Ḥodesh,* as on festivals, a special prayer, *Ya'aleh ve-Yavo* ("May [our remembrance] arise and come . . . before Thee"), is recited during the *Amidah* (silent devotion) and in the Grace after Meals. This prayer mentions the day being commemorated, and includes a request for "deliverance, happiness, grace, kindness, mercy, life, and peace."

    Liturgy

    Since talmudic times it has been customary to recite a short form of the *Hallel* (Psalms of praise) on *Rosh Ḥodesh.* The complete *Hallel* is not said because work is not absolutely prohibited, as on a full festival. There is also a controversy as to whether one recites the normal benediction before reading the *Hallel;* community practices vary in this regard. *Hallel* is not recited on *Rosh Ḥodesh* Tishrei, which is also Rosh ha-Shanah, because on that solemn day when men's lives hang in the balance it is not suitable to recite joyful praises and thanksgiving for redemption.

12

The Torah reading for *Rosh Ḥodesh* describes the sacrifices offered on the New Month. When *Rosh Ḥodesh* falls on a Sabbath, two Torah portions are read; that of the week, and that of the New Month. The *haftarah* reading on such a Sabbath is from Isaiah. It begins, "Thus saith the Lord: The heaven is My throne, and the earth My footstool," and ends, "And it shall come to pass, that from one new moon to another, and from one Sabbath to another, shall all the flesh come to worship before Me, saith the Lord."

Psalm 104, known by its opening words, *Barekhi Nafshi* ("Bless the Lord, O my soul"), is recited after the morning service and, in the Sephardi rite, before the evening service as well. This psalm is regarded as one of the most beautiful examples of ancient Hebrew poetry. A magnificent expression of monotheistic belief, its central theme is the glorification of God as the Creator of the universe, whose majesty and beauty testify to His wisdom.

An 18th century Dutch illustrated *Megillah*. The figures around the text are the zodiacal signs for the months.

Because *Rosh Ḥodesh* is a day of joy, it is forbidden to fast on it; a funeral held on that day has an abbreviated service, and the *Taḥanun* (supplication) prayer is not recited. The *Shulḥan Arukh,* the Jewish code of laws, considers it desirable to partake of a festive meal on that day.

Religious circles in Israel have granted *Rosh Ḥodesh* a measure of official recognition as a contemporary holiday. The network of religious schools under government supervision mark the day with special assembly programs, and religious women's organizations hold study sessions for their members on *Rosh Ḥodesh*. A special program called "A Good Month" is broadcast by the national television network on the Saturday night preceding the new month. However, attempts to recognize *Rosh Ḥodesh* as a full public holiday have not yet met with success.

2. ISRAEL INDEPENDENCE DAY

The sense of Jewish peoplehood, the awareness of a common heritage and history, is perhaps nowhere more clearly reflected than in the adoption of Israel Independence Day, Yom ha-Aẓma'ut, by Jewish communities throughout the world as a modern festival, one of the holiday observances of the Jewish calendar.

Yom ha-Aẓma'ut is celebrated on the fifth of Iyyar, the anniversary, according to the Hebrew calendar, of the day in 5708 (May 14, 1948) when Israel's Declaration of Independence was promulgated and the State of Israel was established. It was legally declared a public holiday in Israel in 1949. When the day falls on a Sabbath or a Friday, Yom Ha-Aẓma'ut is celebrated on the preceding Thursday, in order to avoid violation of the Sabbath.

Ceremonies and Celebrations
The Independence Day festivities are inaugurated on the eve of

14

the holiday by a solemn ceremony on Mount Herzl, Jerusalem,
the grave-site of Theodor Herzl, through whose efforts the vision
of a Jewish Homeland was translated into political reality. The
Speaker of the Knesset (Israel's parliament) ushers in the festival
by lighting a torch; then, in turn, twelve torches are kindled,
symbolizing the tribes of Israel. The torch-lighters are chosen
each year to represent aspects of Israel's modern history and its
struggle for statehood and survival. The ceremony is concluded
by a gun salute, corresponding in number of rounds with the
years of independence.

An Independence Day
fireworks display in Tel
Aviv (right). The flame
is lit on Mt. Herzl in
Jerusalem at the end
of Yom ha-Zikkaron to
signify the beginning
of Yom ha-Azma'ut
(below).

For the first 20 years of the state's existence, and again on the twenty-fifth anniversary, the main official event marking Independence Day was an armed forces parade. In addition, the President of the State holds a reception which is attended by the heads of diplomatic missions. Another reception honors soldiers of the Israel Defense Forces who have distinguished themselves in the performance of their duties. On this day, too, the prestigious Israel Prize is awarded to citizens who have earned public recognition or made outstanding contributions in literature, music, art, science, Bible studies, history, sociology, and other fields.

Popular Celebrations

In contrast to the solemnity of the official ceremonies marking Independence Day, the public celebrates with informal gaiety. The eve of Yom ha-Azma'ut is marked by firework displays, dancing in the streets, parties, and organized open-air entertainment. The day itself is one of picnics and trips, sports events, theatrical performances and dance pageants. The International Bible Contest for Jewish Youth is held on this day. The contestants, who are the winners of national competitions held in Israel and in Jewish communities abroad, compete before a packed hall, and a nationwide radio audience follows the questions and answers with the greatest interest. A Hebrew Song Festival is also held, with new songs, written for the occasion, competing for popular approval.

The annual Israel Song Festival on Independence Day, 1972.

16

Religious Practices

Efforts are being made to evolve ways of celebrating Israel Independence Day within the framework of Jewish religious tradition. The day is recognized as a religious festival, to be marked by a festive meal *(se'udat mitzvah)* at home, and by special prayers in the synagogue.

In 1949 the Israel Chief Rabbinate formulated a pattern of prayers to be recited on Yom ha-Azma'ut. The festive evening service *(Ma'ariv)* is introduced by Psalms 107, 97 and 98, all songs of thanksgiving to God. Psalm 107 begins: *Evening Service*

O give thanks unto the Lord, for He is good,
For His mercy endureth for ever.
So let the redeemed of the Lord say
Whom He hath redeemed from the hand of the adversary;
And gathered them out of the lands,
From the east and from the west,
From the north and from the sea.

The evening service concludes with the sounding of the *shofar,* and with a petition: "May it be Thy will, that as we have been deemed worthy to witness the beginning of redemption, so also may we be deemed worthy to hear the *shofar* announcing the Messiah, speedily in our days."

The theme of redemption, which is at the core of the religious interpretation of Yom ha-Azma'ut, is an ancient concept in Judaism. The rabbis taught that the dream of redemption is one of the seven basic values which existed before the world was created, and which provided the basis for the fashioning of man. *Redemption*

At the very heart of Judaism is the covenant, entered into by God and Abraham, and then by his descendants, a covenant which promised them a land in which they could develop into a kingdom of priests and a holy people. This promise first saw

17

realization after the Exodus from Egypt and the settlement in the Land of Israel. Following the destruction of the Temple and the exile of the people, the concept of redemption remained rooted in the hearts of the Jews. It was further developed by the rabbis, and found an expression in the daily laws and customs of Judaism. The hope of redemption has sustained the Jewish community in periods of great suffering and persecution.

David Ben-Gurion reading Israel's Declaration of Independence, May 14, 1948.

The reality of Israel's political existence grew out of the strong religious belief in the return of the people of Israel to the Land of Israel, and out of the pioneering efforts of small numbers of pragmatic idealists, who sought to bring about the redemption of the land.

18

The theme of redemption runs through Israel's Proclamation of Independence, which was approved by the People's Council of the Jewish community in Palestine on May 14, 1948, and which declared the establishment of the State of Israel.

Commemorative coin issued on Israel's 25th Independence Day (1973). One side indicates the value and the other reproduces part of the Declaration of Independence.

The Declaration of Independence begins by explaining the justification for the establishment of the Jewish state at that moment in history. It recalls the shaping of the Jewish people and their culture in the Land of Israel, their unbroken attachment to the land throughout the centuries of their dispersion, and their return in recent generations to found a thriving and self-reliant society. The declaration also makes note of contemporary reality, of the problems emerging from the events of the Holocaust, and of the need to provide a safe haven for the ingathering of the Jewish exiles.

It continues with a historical record. The right of the Jewish people to national restoration in their land was voiced by the First Zionist Congress, acknowledged in the Balfour Declaration, confirmed in the League of Nations Mandate, and irrevocably recognized by the United Nations. Thus, "by virtue of our natural and historic right, and of the resolution of the General Assembly of the United Nations," the People's Council proclaimed the establishment of "a Jewish State in the Land of Israel — the State of Israel."

The morning service *(Shaharit)* for Independence Day includes the introductory Psalms recited on Sabbaths and festivals, *Nishmat, Hallel,* and the reading from the Prophets that is recited on the last day of Passover in the Diaspora — Isaiah's vision of the End of Days when peace will reign, "For the earth shall be full of the knowledge of the Lord as the waters cover the sea", and the dispersed of Israel "will be gathered together from the four corners of the earth." The two latter prayers are not accompanied by their respective benedictions. *Tahanun* (the penitential prayer) is omitted, as on all festive days.

This order of services is still rather fluid. Some religious elements in Israel, particularly the Religious Kibbutz Movement and the Israel Defense Forces rabbinate, have felt this order of service to be inadequate to the historic nature of the occasion. They have urged the inclusion of the *she-heheyanu* benediction recited on all festivals, and the reading of a special portion of the Torah. (Some suggestions were the seventh chapter of Deuteronomy which begins, "When the Lord thy God shall bring thee into the land whither thou goest to possess it," or the thirtieth chapter of Deuteronomy, " . . . that then the Lord thy God will turn thy captivity, and have compassion upon thee, and will return and gather thee from all the peoples, wither the Lord thy God hath scattered thee. . . .") On the other hand, extreme Orthodox circles objected to any changes in the liturgy, and to the conversion of Independence Day into a full religious festival.

Despite the lack of uniformity in Israel regarding the ritual practices of Yom ha-Azma'ut, the Chief Rabbinate's order of service has been printed in two standard editions of Israel prayerbooks. In addition, an anthology of religious readings, prayers and customs for Independence Day has been approved.

The Religious Kibbutz Movement (Ha-Kibbutz ha-Dati) has printed its own prayerbook for this day. It incorporates the recital of *she-heḥeyanu* after reciting a festival *kiddush,* and the reading of *Al ha-Nissim* (the prayer of thanks for miracles, also read on Purim and Ḥanukkah) in the *Amidah.*

Many Jewish communities in the Diaspora have incorporated *In the Diaspora* some of these readings and prayers into a special service held either on Israel Independence Day, or on the Sabbath preceding it. Their practices are far from uniform. A Hebrew-English Prayerbook issued in London under the imprimatur of the Chief Rabbi of England includes the order of service established by Israel's Chief Rabbinate. The Weekday Prayerbook of the Conservative movement in the United States includes a newly-composed *Al ha-Nissim* prayer for Yom ha-Aẓma'ut. Virtually all the recently published Liberal and Reform prayerbooks in Europe and the United States include a prayer for the State of Israel.

Civic groups within Jewish communities throughout the Diaspora also hold public commemorative gatherings marking Israel Independence Day.

Among the growing number of Independence Day rituals that have been adopted by various Jewish communities, one may mention the practice of proclaiming the number of years since the establishment of the State, followed by the sounding of the *shofar* in the evening service. The text is adapted from the proclamation of the years which have passed since the destruction of the Temple, which is made in Sephardi and Yemenite synagogues on the ninth of Av. The text reads: "Hear ye, our brethren! Today . . . years have elapsed since the beginning of our redemption, marked by the establishment of the State."

Remembrance Day

The joyous festivities of Independence Day are balanced by a day of solemn commemoration for all those who have, over the years, fallen in defense of Israel's security, and whose sacrifice made independence possible. Remembrance Day (Yom ha-Zikkaron), which is the day preceding Yom ha-Aẓma'ut, is marked by special prayer services, visits to cemeteries, and memorial assemblies which are jointly civil, military and religious in nature.

The commemoration begins at sunset of the preceding day, with a minute-long siren blast, and an opening ceremony at the Western Wall in Jerusalem. A bereaved parent presents a torch to the President, who lights a memorial flame for those who died in Israel's defense. Israelis throughout the country light memorial candles in their homes at the same time, and thousands of memorial lights are kindled at parade grounds and public buildings, with guards of honor stationed beside them. By law, all places of entertainment are closed on that evening.

During Remembrance Day itself, memorial ceremonies are held at public monuments to the fallen and in the military cemeteries throughout the country, with the members of the Cabinet in attendance. All flags are flown at half-mast.

The Israel Chief Rabbinate has prescribed special prayers for Yom ha-Zikkaron and for the Sabbath that precedes it. These include the recital of Psalms 9: "For the leader, on the death of the son," and 144: "Blessed be the Lord, my Rock, who traineth my hands for war and my fingers for battle."

The solemn character of Remembrance Day concludes with a siren blast at nightfall, as the stars appear, to usher in Israel Independence Day with its festivities.

Yom Yerushalayim
Echoes of the festivities of Yom ha-Aẓma'ut recur 23 days later, on the twenty-eighth of Iyyar, when all Israel again celebrates what has been declared the newest holiday of the Jewish calendar — Yom Yerushalayim (Jerusalem Day).

On the twenty-eighth of Iyyar in 1967 (Wednesday, June 7), the third day of the Six-Day War, Israeli forces broke through the

Lions' Gate of the Old City wall, entered the area to which Jews had been denied access since 1948, and captured the Old City. The old and the new sections of Jerusalem were officially joined, and united Jerusalem again became the capital of the nation, and the functioning heart within a living Jewish state.

The Israel Rabbinate has proclaimed Yom Yerushalayim to be a day of thanksgiving, and has directed that the *Shaḥarit* (morning) service that day include the *Hallel,* Psalm 107, and a verse-by-verse reading of the "Song of the Sea," which praises God for His triumph over Israel's enemies. The day is also to be celebrated with a joyous, festive meal. Despite the fact that Yom Yerushalayim falls within the mourning period of the *Omer* (see page 25), the restrictions of that period are lifted "because of the importance of the miracle which the Lord caused for His people Israel in the liberation of Jerusalem."

Nonetheless, the celebration of Yom Yerushalayim is a blend of solemnity and joy. The day begins with a thanksgiving service at the Western Wall attended by thousands of Jerusalemites, where eighteen torches are lit in memory of the soldiers who fell in the battle for Jerusalem. Throughout Israel, Jews participate in both memorial services and festive gatherings. As with Yom ha-Azma'ut, there is a bitter-sweet flavor to the commemoration of Yom Yerushalayim.

Jerusalem divided — before the Six Day War.

23

Neither a day observed by prayer and ritual in the synagogue, nor a home festival marked by ceremony and traditional foods, Lag ba-Omer is a holiday celebrated in forest and field, a day marked by bonfires and archery contests, haircuts and weddings. It is a festival whose origins have been lost in the mists of early history. But it has been kept alive by the persistence of the Jewish people who have continued to observe the customs associated with it, even though the reasons for these customs have long been forgotten.

A typical Lag ba-Omer scene in Israel.

The name "Lag ba-Omer" merely describes the day on which the holiday falls. *Lag* is the equivalent of 33 in Hebrew letters. The *Omer* is the name given to a period of 49 days between Passover and Shavuot. Thus, Lag ba-Omer is the thirty-third day of the *Omer* period.

24

The counting of the *Omer* period is prescribed in Leviticus, chapter 23, which enjoins the bringing of a sheaf *(Omer)* of the harvest to the Temple priest the day after Passover, and keeping count seven full weeks thereafter. On the fiftieth day, an offering of grain from the new harvest is to be brought to the Temple.

These seven weeks between Passover, which marked the ripening of the barley harvest, and Shavuot, which was the feast of the wheat harvest and of the first fruits, were crucial to the agricultural economy of ancient Israel. The counting of the *Omer* served as an expression of Israel's faith in God's ensuring a fruitful year.

A woodcutting in an 18th century *minhagim* (customs) book, illustrating that haircutting is permitted on Lag ba-Omer.

The Omer Period

Sometime during the talmudic period, the days of the *Omer*-counting took on a character of semi-mourning. The celebration of marriages was prohibited; then haircutting was banned; and later still, the use of musical instruments was forbidden. The reason for the mourning is a subject for many theories.

According to tradition, a terrible plague raged among the students of Rabbi Akiva, a great scholar of the first century, during the period of the *Omer*-counting, killing 24,000 of them. However, while the Talmud makes mention of this plague, it does not say anything about customs of mourning in this regard. Rather, such customs are first recorded only in the eighth century.

The mourning restriction of the *Omer* period are relaxed on the thirty-third day, Lag ba-Omer, which is a day of festivities.

The Thirty-third Day

Lag ba-Omer is first mentioned by name in the 13th century, and is described as the day when "according to a tradition of the the *geonim*" the plague which decimated the students of Rabbi Akiva ceased.

The kabbalists attach particular significance to Lag ba-Omer, for they believe this to be the anniversary of the death of Rabbi Simeon bar Yoḥai, a great scholar and ascetic whom they regard as the author of the central work of Jewish mysticism, the *Zohar*.

Since the 16th or 17th century a great Lag ba-Omer festival has been celebrated at the town of Meron, in Upper Galilee. It is here that tradition locates the tombs of Rabbi Simeon bar Yoḥai and his son Rabbi Eleazar.

The yeshiva built above the tomb of Rabbi Simeon bar Yohai in Meron.

26

According to custom rooted in the distant past, the Hillula ceremonies, which are called a *hillula,* begin with a great gathering in the nearby holy city of Safed, home of the kabalists who taught the mystic book of the *Zohar.* On the eve of the holiday, a procession bearing a Torah scroll proceeds down Safed's winding lanes to Meron, which lies some five miles away in the mountains. There a *yeshivah* stands above the graves of the venerated rabbis.

The participants in the *hillula* recite a special hymn praising Bar Yoḥai and celebrate with feasting, song and dance. As darkness falls, bonfires are lit. Some of the celebrants throw articles of clothing belonging to a person who is sick or in need of divine help into the fire.

For generations, the rabbis have strongly protested the festivities, holding that it is not fitting to observe the anniversary of a person's death in this manner. They have also tried to stop the burning of clothing, viewing this practice as having undesirable magical connotations, and as exemplifying the sin of purposeless waste (in modern terminology: conspicuous consumption). However, the ingrained folk customs have proven stronger than rabbinic sermons!

A unique custom associated with Lag ba-Omer in Meron is The First
Haircut the practice, among the Orthodox community, of giving three-year-old boys their first haircut *(ḥalakah)* on that day. This practice goes back at least to the 16th century, for the great kabbalist Isaac Luria "brought his small son there together with his whole family, and they cut his hair there according to the well-known custom, and they spent a day of feasting and celebration."

After the child's hair is cut, the locks are thrown into a bonfire, and the parents distribute wine and cakes to those participating in the festivities. This custom undoubtedly was originally a pagan rite of magic, in which part of a person's body, in this case his hair, was sacrified to appease evil spirits and guard the body itself from their wrath. However, the Jewish gift of "Judaizing", customs and ceremonies borrowed from other groups absorbed this magical rite; for the emphasis in the haircutting ceremony at Meron is not on the burning of the child's hair, but rather on the long earlocks that remain on his head after all the rest of his hair has been cut. At the end of the haircutting ceremony, the three-year-old is unmistakably an Orthodox Jewish child!

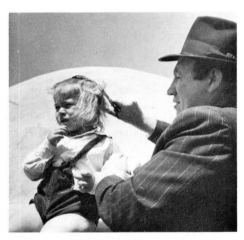

A three-year-old's first haircut at the Lag ba-Omer celebrations in Meron (left). Hasidim dancing at Meron, on Lag ba-Omer. Note the children before their haircuts (below).

Customs

Since the period of the 49 days, from the second day of Passover *Marriages* to Shavuot, is a time of mourning, joyous occasions are not observed during those seven weeks. Only on Lag ba-Omer are the mourning restrictions lifted. Thus, that day is generally marked by scores of marriages.

Theodore Gaster, a noted student of comparative religions, points out that many cultures considered it unlucky to solemnize marriages during the early spring, before the harvest of the new year, when the economic fate of the community was still an unknown factor. He cites as examples such folk sayings as "If you marry in Lent, you will live to repent," and "Marry in May, rue for aye."

The superstition against entering into marriage prior to the harvest festival is also found in ancient Rome. The Roman poet Ovid, who recorded the legends and customs of his time, explained that marriages were not solemnized in May because that was the month of the *Lemuria,* when the souls of the departed returned to wander over the earth and disturb the peace of the living. Funeral rites were held to appease the spirits, and marrying during this month was considered to be most unlucky. In an interesting parallel with Jewish custom, the Roman period of superstitious fear lasted for 32 days, and its conclusion was celebrated with a festival on the 33rd day.

In countries of the Diaspora, for many centuries, it was *Bows and* customary for Jewish children to spend days before Lag ba-Omer *Arrows* fashioning bows and arrows from branches of bushes or young trees, and to go out into the field or forest to hold archery contests. It is, indeed, difficult to understand how such a custom arose within the Jewish community which has always disapproved of hunting as a sport.

Scholars interpret the use of bows and arrows as a reminder of the students of Rabbi Akiva who died in great numbers during the *Omer* period, and were spared on the 33rd day. Rabbi Akiva

(c. 50–135) was not only the foremost scholar of his age, but was also a patriot and a martyr. In 132 c.e., a full-scale revolt against Rome broke out in Israel under the leadership of Bar Kokhba. Rabbi Akiva supported the revolt, and viewed Bar Kokhba as a messiah who would liberate Israel from its oppressors. It is suggested that Rabbi Akiva gave more than moral support to the revolt, and that the many trips he took to meet with scholars and collect funds for the poor may have had the additional purpose of helping to raise support for Bar Kokhba.

It has also been suggested that the reference in the Talmud to the death of large numbers of Rabbi Akiva's students is a veiled report of their unsuccessful battle against Rome during the Bar Kokhba rebellion. It is possible that Bar Kokhba's (and Akiva's) men suffered an overwhelming defeat by the Romans during the weeks between Passover and Shavuot. On the 33rd day of the *Omer*-counting, however, they may have enjoyed an important though brief, triumph – possibly, the recapture of Jerusalem, for which special coins were struck. Thus the use of bows and arrows commemorates their victory.

Other scholars trace the custom to a legend that the rainbow, a symbol of God's promise not to destroy the world (see Genesis 9:11-17) did not have to appear during the lifetime of Rabbi Simeon bar Yoḥai, because he was such a saintly man. Notwithstanding these explanations, the origin of the custom may, in this case again, be pagan. A common practice existed in many cultures of shooting arrows at "evil spirits" on days when they were believed to be especially active. One such day was May Day, and even in this century, in some rural areas of England, archery contests are held at this time of the year.

Lag ba-Omer is very much a children's and students' holiday *In Israel* in Israel. Elementary and high schools are closed, and sports competitions and outings to the countryside are planned for pupils. The university campuses celebrate "Students'-Day." This is a modern expression of the medieval "scholars' festival" which was celebrated by rabbinical students in commemoration of Rabbi Akiva's students having been saved from the plague.

Throughout the country, on the eve of Lag ba-Omer, the darkness is pierced by thousands of bonfires which send up bright signals from empty lots, fields and hillsides. The children who have lit them cannot tell you why bonfires "belong" to Lag ba-Omer, but modern scholars suggest that they too go back to the time of the Bar Kokhba revolt.

When the Romans incorporated the land of Israel into their empire, one of their first acts was to prohibit the lighting of the fires signalling the beginning of the new month (see page 3). By forbidding the lighting of these fires, they impressed upon the Jews that they were no longer a sovereign people, able to establish their own religious laws. Therefore, when Bar Kokhba instigated a revolt against Rome, one of the first things his followers did was to renew the lighting of the signal fires.

The story of the Bar Kokhba revolt was played down in subsequent centuries, say these scholars, because it was dangerous to remind the governments of the various countries in which the Jews lived that they had been rebellious. But in the hearts of the folk, the connection between the rebellion, Bar Kokhba, and Simeon bar Yoḥai was kept alive — symbolized in the Lag ba-Omer bonfires.

4. TU BE-AV

Tu be-Av is a minor holiday which was instituted during the period of the Second Temple, and was apparently unable to maintain a hold on the popular imagination, so that it is largely ignored in the calendar of Jewish festivals.

The name Tu be-Av literally means "the fifteenth day of the month of Av" (July—August). In Hebrew, the word *tu* is the equivalent of the number 15. It consists of the letters *tet* and *vav*,

31

equal to nine and six, respectively. (Logically, the letters *yod* and *heh* — ten and five — should constitute the number 15, but these letters spell the name of God, and are not used for secular purposes.) Thus, Tu (= 15) Be (= "in") Av is the fifteenth day of Av.

The Day of the Wood Offering

When the Temple stood, there were nine different dates during the year when specified families were given the privilege of bringing offerings of wood to be used for the sacrificial fires on the altar. On the fifteenth of Av, which fell in mid-summer, the priests, the Levites, and all those families who were not sure from which tribe they had descended were permitted to bring a wood offering. From this day onward, no more wood was chopped for the Temple, because the sun was no longer strong enough to dry the fresh-cut logs sufficiently so that the fire would not smoke.

The importance placed on the wood-offering is reflected in a story related in the Talmud about a family from the town of Netofah, whom the rabbis praised for their efforts in obtaining wood for the Temple altar. It happened once, that the Jews were forbidden by the authorities to bring wood for the altar fires in the Temple. Guards were placed on the roads to enforce this decree. The Netofah family took logs and made them into ladders which they carried on their shoulders as they set out for Jerusalem. When they were stopped by the guards, they explained that they were going to use the ladders to climb up to dovecotes to capture young pigeons. Once past the guards, they dismantled the ladders and brought the logs to Jerusalem.

Festival of the Vineyards

A tradition recorded in the time of the Mishnah linked Tu be-Av with Yom Kippur. According to the Mishnah, in ancient times these two days were the happiest of the Jewish festivals, for on them the maidens of Jerusalem dressed themselves in white clothes (which they borrowed, so that the daughters of poor families need not be ashamed of not having suitable dresses) and went out to dance in the vineyards. It is probable that the two days were linked together because Tu be-Av, which falls in July-August, marked the beginning of the grape harvest and the season of wine-making, while Yom Kippur (late September—October) marked its end.

Primitive Origins
The Talmud offers half a dozen additional reasons why Tu be-Av was celebrated as a minor holiday, which would seem to indicate that the true origin of the festival was not known. Some scholars believe that it was originally a pagan observance of mid-summer day, just as Tu bi-Shevat originally marked mid-winter day (see page 63).

Because Tu be-Av is a minor festival, the *Taḥanun* prayer is omitted from the daily service, and no eulogy is said at a funeral held on that day.

Kibbutz Festivals
In recent years attempts have been made in various kibbutzim to revive this festival. Called *Ḥagigat ha-Keramim,* (the "Festival of the Vineyards"), the celebrations include music, dancing, poetry and love songs.

Another festival having its origin in the kibbutz is *Ḥagigat ha-Gez,* the Sheepshearing Festival, which originated in the 1920s in the Valley of Jezreel. It is celebrated only in kibbutzim that own flocks, and symbolizes the joy of the shepherd when the shearing is finished. The last sheep is ceremonially shorn to the accompaniment of singing and dancing. Short plays are performed, usually based on the theme of I Samuel chapter 25, and displays of woolen goods and art on pastoral themes are held.

Kibbutzim have also sought to instill modern pastoral motifs

33

into the three pilgrim festivals, Passover, (the Spring Festival), Shavuot (the Festival of the First Fruits), and Sukkot (the Harvest Festival), and have created new ceremonies appropriate to these themes.

5. HANUKKAH

The festival of Ḥanukkah, which begins of the twenty-fifth day of Kislev (December) and lasts for eight days, is one of the brightest holidays of the Jewish year. Until the addition of Yom ha-Azma'ut to the Jewish calendar of holidays, it had the distinction of being the only Jewish festival based on a specific historic event that could be dated with accuracy. Ḥanukkah means (Feast of) Dedication; it is also known as the Feast of Lights. These names reflect the development of different interpretations of the holiday in ancient times. In fact, Ḥanukkah is a holiday whose celebration has taken on additional meaning for Jews in the 20th century.

Ḥanukkah in the Westerbork Concentration Camp, 1942 (left). Plaster fragments showing a *menorah* found in excavations in the Jewish Quarter of the Old City of Jerusalem dating back to the time of Herod (37-4 b.c.e.).

Origins

The events from which the festival of Ḥanukkah emerged are related in the First and Second Books of Maccabees. These are historical works which provide the main source of information for events in Palestine during the second century b.c.e. Both books have come down to us in the Greek language, but scholars believe that the First Book was originally written in Hebrew. (There are two additional Books of Maccabees, dating from a somewhat later period, but these are works of philosophy, sermons and legends, rather than historical narratives.)

Books of Maccabees

Judas Maccabeus ; enamel plaque, France, 16th century.

The First Book of Maccabees tells of the conquest of most of the Near East and Asia by Alexander the Great in the 4th century b.c.e., and the division of his kingdom among several rulers after his death. The area that was Judea became part of the Seleucid (Syrian Greek) kingdom. In 175 b.c.e. Antiochus IV Epiphanes ascended the Seleucid throne, and it was his reign and decrees which sparked a rebellion among the inhabitants of Judea, and marked a turning point in Jewish history.

The Second Book of Maccabees covers many of the same events, but presents them in a different order, and concentrates its attention on the deeds of Judah Maccabee, the heroic figure of the Jewish revolt. The author of the book may have been a contemporary of Judah Maccabee, for several incidents seem to have been written by an eyewitness to the events.

35

The Books of Maccabees were not considered sacred, and were not included in the biblical "canon". Books of this sort came to be known as "hidden away", or apocryphal. The early Christians (that is, the Catholic and Greek Orthodox rituals) included the apochryphal writings among their holy books, and these narratives occupy a place in their Bible between the Hebrew Scriptures and the Christian Gospels. However, they are not part of the Protestant Bible.

History

Antiochus Epiphanes, king of the Seleucid kingdom was an *Antiochus* ambitious ruler. His kingdom was composed of a patchwork of *Epiphanes* small national groups, each quite different from the other. In the ancient Near East, church and state were frequently synony- mous; the sense of nationhood was bound up in a particular religion. Thus, when Antiochus sought to strengthen his kingdom, he imposed laws on the various national groups under his control that would replace local beliefs and rituals with Greek gods and practices. In the uniformity of religion and culture, he saw the means to unite his kingdom.

Antiochus paid particular attention to the Jews, who had remained faithful to their belief in the One God. He appointed a series of High Priests who had strong leanings toward hellenistic (Greek-oriented) ideas. Under their guidance, Greek influence spread in Jerusalem, particularly among the aristocracy. A Greek-style community was set up within the walls of Jerusalem. The young priests turned from service in the Temple to partici- pation in Greek athletics. Hebrew names were abandoned in favor of Greek names such as Alexander, Helena, Aristobolus. A process of assimilation into the majority Greek culture was under way.

But it would seem that this was not sufficient for Antiochus. He instituted a series of laws which compelled the Jews, under penalty of death, to depart from the laws of their fathers, and to

36

cease living by the laws of God. Further, the sanctuary in Jerusalem was to be polluted, and converted into a temple to the glory of Zeus Olympus.

The severe nature of these laws has puzzled students of the Hellenistic Period. This extreme effort at hellenization was not applied by Antiochus to any of the non-Jewish groups under his rule. Perhaps he saw religious oppression as the only means of achieving political stability in Palestine, since the stubborn belief in the One God and the loyalty of Jews to their religious laws and tradition stood out uniquely among the peoples in his empire. There is also a possibility that these laws may not have been an expression of a rational policy. The king's own contemporaries referred to him as Epimanes ("madman"), instead of Epiphanes, and like tyrants within our own memories, his personal instability undoubtedly influenced his policies.

The extreme decrees of Antiochus, which forbade the Jews to worship God, ordered them to bow down before the idol of Zeus which was erected in the Temple, and commanded them to eat the forbidden flesh of pigs, met with resistance on the part of a small, but valiant group of Jews.

The leader of the uprising was Mattathias of the Hasmonean family, a priest from the village of Modi'in. The First Book of Maccabees and the history of the Jews written by Josephus, in the first century, relate that a company of Greek officers arrived at Modi'in with the intention of forcing its inhabitants to sacrifice to idols. Since Mattathias was held in great respect by the villagers, he was ordered to begin the sacrificial offerings. Mattathias refused to do so, but another Jew stepped forward to fulfill the officer's command. Mattathias reacted by killing both the Jew and the Greek officer. He then raised the rallying cry proclaimed centuries earlier by Moses when he discovered the Israelites rejoicing with the Golden Calf: "All those who remain faithful to the Lord, join with me! "

Together with his sons — Judah, Simeon, Johanan, Eleazar

and Jonathan — and a number of like-minded Jews, Mattathias went into hiding in the desert and mountain area of Judea. From bases of refuge they initiated a series of guerrilla attacks on the Greek units.

Even while the Hasmoneans (as Mattathias and his sons were known) waged military war against the Greeks, they also fought a religious battle against those of their fellow-Jews whose spirit had

The Hasmoneans

"The Hasmoneans," a panel on the outdoor *menorah* presented by the British Parliament to the Israel Knesset. Designed by Benno Elkan.

been broken by the Greeks and who had adopted Greek ways. Both the First Book of Maccabees and Josephus state that Mattathias rounded up all the children brought up under the influence of enforced hellenization, and had them circumcised.

Mattathias led the rebellion for one year. Before his death, he appointed two of his five sons to continue as leaders of the revolt. Judah Maccabee was declared military commander, and Simeon became the Hasmonean counselor.

Judah Maccabee is famed as one of the great warriors of history. He had exceptional military talent, and his valor was legendary. The name "Maccabee" may mean "hammer" and refer to his great strength; another explanation is that it is formed from the initial letters of the words *Mi Kamokha Ba-elim Y.H.W.H.*, "who is like unto Thee among the gods, O Lord." *Judah Maccabee*

Because of the size and strength of the Greek army, Judah's strategy, at first, was to avoid involvement with the regular units, and to attack from ambush. In time, however, his own fighting ranks expanded, and his outstanding tactical skill enabled him to win a series of battles against a regular army of far superior force, led by experienced officers.

Finally Judah was able to enter Jerusalem at the head of his army. They marched into the Temple compound, to find the holy area defiled. The Jewish soldiers, under Judah's guidance, proceeded to purify the Temple. The old altar, which had been polluted, was demolished, and a new one built. Judah then had new holy vessels — a candelabrum, an altar for incense, a table, and curtains — made. On the twenty-fifth of Kislev of the year 148 of the Seleucid era, corresponding to 164 b.c.e., he rededicated the Temple.

The First Ḥanukkah

The day on which Judah Maccabee rededicated the Temple, the twenty-fifth of Kislev, was probably chosen because it coincided with the third anniversary of the decree issued by Antiochus

Epiphanes that idolatrous sacrifices should be offered upon the holy altar in the Temple.

Now the new altar was to be consecrated. The daily service of sacrifices was to be renewed, accompanied by song, the playing of musical instruments, and the chanting of *Hallel*. The First

Festival of Dedication

Early 18th century copperplate engraving depicting the Temple altar and sacrifice. It is one of a series of illustrations in a Hebrew - Latin edition of the Mishnah.

Book of Maccabees makes no mention of any special dedication customs or rituals. It does say that the celebrations lasted for eight days, and that Judah decreed that they were to be commemorated as days of rejoicing and a festival of dedication in all future generations.

Detail from a 15th century Hebrew illuminated manuscript from northern Italy, the *Rothschild Miscellany*, showing Judith holding Holofernes' head. The warrior's costume is typical of the Italian Renaissance period.

Silver Ḥanukkah lamp from Augsburg, Germany, 18th century. The legs are in the form of bears. In relief are the blessings in Hebrew (right) and the prayer *Hanerot halalu anu madli-im*, "We kindle these lights . . ." The Temple candelabrum in the center is flanked by Moses and Aaron, while the standing figures include Judah Maccabee and Judith.

Children in a Jerusalem kindergarten preparing for Ḥanukkah.

Moroccan Ḥanukkah candelabra from the 17th, 18th and 19th centuries.

In the Second Book of Maccabees, the main aspects of Ḥanukkah are related in similar fashion. The book adds, however, that the eight days of dedication followed the pattern of King Solomon's consecration of his Temple (which had been dedicated during the eight-day Festival of Sukkot), being celebrated "with gladness, like the Feast of Sukkot, remembering how, not long before, during the Feast of Sukkot, they had been wandering like wild beasts in the mountains and the caves. So, bearing wands wreathed with leaves and fair boughs and palms, they offered hymns of praise."

Judah and his followers may have wished to dramatize the rededication of the Temple by copying the ritual followed by Solomon. But it is also possible that since the Hasmonean guerrilla bands had been unable to observe Sukkot at its proper time, they celebrated a "postponed" holiday by bringing palm branches to the Temple during the rededication ceremony.

In neither of the Books of Maccabees is there any mention of *Festival of* that aspect of Ḥanukkah which now symbolizes the holiday, and *Lights* which indeed constitutes its main ritual observance — the kindling of the Ḥanukkah lights. The lighting of the *menorah* is noted, but that was part of the daily ritual in the Temple, and was not a special act of dedication.

When, two centuries later, Josephus records the victory of the Hasmoneans and the rededication of the altar, he does not call the festival by the name of "Ḥanukkah", but writes: "From that time onward unto this day, we celebrate the festival, calling it 'Lights.' " Evidently Josephus did not know why the festival had acquired that name, for he resorts to the lame explanation that the right to serve God came to the people unexpectedly, like a sudden light!

One explanation of the name "Festival of Lights" is based on the above-mentioned connection between Ḥanukkah and Sukkot. The eight-day festival of Sukkot, includes a ceremony known as "the rejoicing of the place of water-drawing" *(Simḥat Bet ha-*

41

Sho'evah). Huge golden candlesticks were lit in the Temple court on these occasions, "and there was not a courtyard in Jerusalem that did not reflect the light of the *Bet ha-Sho'evah.*" Moreover, "men of piety and good works used to dance before them with burning torches in their hands, singing songs and praises." It is possible that when the Hasmoneans rededicated the Temple along the lines of a Sukkot observance, this ceremony of the water-drawing, with its lights and festivities, was included, and served as the origin of the name "Festival of Lights".

Some scholars of comparative religion suggest that the practice of kindling lights at this time of the year pre-dated the rededication festival, and may represent an adaptation of the familiar pagan custom of lighting fires at the time of the winter solstice, when the days are just beginning to grow longer.

Several traditions have been transmitted to explain the reason for kindling lights on the eight nights of Hanukkah. One states that the Hasmoneans could not use the candelabrum in the

Miracle of the Oil

Ceramic oil lamp decorated with a *menorah* in relief.
Alexandria, 4th century c.e.

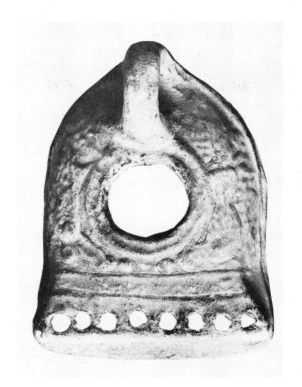

A clay oil lamp with light spouts, perhaps for Ḥanukkah use; Erez Israel, Talmud period.

Temple since the Greeks had defiled it. They, therefore, took iron spits, covered them with zinc, and used them as a candelabrum. During the second century, in fact, the sages taught that the candelabrum of the early Hasmoneans was not made of gold.

But the most popular tradition regarding the Ḥanukkah lights is that of the miracle of the oil. It relates that when the Hasmoneans entered the Temple, they discovered that the Greeks had defiled all the oil, except for one small jar. That jar contained enough oil to keep the candelabrum burning for one day only. However, a miracle occurred; the candelabrum lights burned for the eight days it took to prepare fresh, pure oil.

A German *menorah* of the 19th century. The eight separate tin "chairs" hold oil, and a "chair" was probably added daily.

In a sense, the story of the jar of oil helped to preserve Ḥanukkah as a festival, particularly in the period following the destruction of the Temple (70 c.e.). The Jewish rebellion against Rome had ended in catastrophe — destruction and exile. The Jews did not want their conquerors to think them still rebellious, and they played down the story of the Hasmonean revolt and victory.

During this period, the miracle of the oil lent weight to a religious interpretation of the holiday. Ḥanukkah began to assume a broader significance than the celebration of a military victory, or the hope of regaining independence. It came to represent the survival of Jewish culture and religion, and the continuance of Jewish life, wherever the Jew lived, even as part of a minority group.

In recent years, Ḥanukkah has reassumed a nationalistic interpretation, in addition to retaining its religious significance (see page 59).

Halakhah

In the Talmud

Tractate Shabbat of the Babylonian Talmud includes a discussion of the laws of Ḥanukkah. The major motivation for kindling the lights is the desire "to proclaim the miracle". The Talmud establishes that the Ḥanukkah lamp should be kindled soon after sunset. "The lamp should be placed outside the entrance of the house. If a person lives on an upper storey, it should be set on the window nearest to the street. If he is in fear of the gentiles, the lamp may be placed inside the inner entrance of the house, and in times of danger, the precept is fulfilled by setting it on the table."

Because of the importance of publicizing the miracle, if a man of limited means has to choose between purchasing oil for the Ḥanukkah lights and wine for *kiddush*, he is to buy the oil. So that the miracle may be known to all, the lights are kindled before any member of the household, adult or child, goes to sleep.

Women are also obliged to kindle the Ḥanukkah lamp, since they were included in the miracle.

The lamp may be filled with any kind of oil, but olive oil is preferred. The quantity should be sufficient for the lamp to remain lit at least half an hour. Nowadays, when it is common custom to light candles, one must choose a candle that will burn for at least half an hour.

The Talmud also records a difference of opinion between the two great scholars, Hillel and Shammai (second half of first century b.c.e.) regarding the kindling of the Ḥanukkah lights.

The law of lighting on Ḥanukkah requires that one light be kindled in each house; the zealous require one light for each person; the extremely zealous add a light for each person each night. According to the School of Shammai, "On the first day, eight lights should be kindled; thereafter they should be progressively reduced," while the School of Hillel held that, "On the first night one light should be kindled, thereafter they should be progressively increased." Shammai's argument was based on the model of a fixed amount of oil which existed on the first night of the holiday, and which grew less with each succeeding night, until it was used up on the eighth night. Hillel reasoned that one does not lessen the sanctity of the holiday each night, but rather adds to it.

The rule established by Hillel of kindling one flame the first night, and adding one light on each successive night until eight lights are kindled on the last night of the holiday, is the one which has been adopted as the normative Jewish practice. A mnemonic device to remind one of this decision is found in the name of the holiday: the initial letters of the words in the Hebrew phrase "eight candles, and the *halakhah* (law) is according to Hillel" form the word Ḥanukkah.

(The rabbis, who enjoyed word games, also read the word Ḥanukkah as "Ḥanu-kah," which may be translated as "they rested on the twenty-fifth," since the number 25 is written with the Hebrew letters *kaf* (20) and *heh* (5). This is a reference to the completion of Judah Maccabee's labors and the dedication of the Temple on the twenty-fifth of Kislev.)

The Talmud teaches that the Ḥanukkah lamp and its lights *The Shammash* may not serve any practical purpose. For that reason, a *shammash,* or "servant" light is used to kindle the eight Ḥanukkah lights. It is left burning so that, should one happen to benefit from the light of the Ḥanukkah lamp for any purpose, the use may be ascribed to the *shammash,* rather than to the Ḥanukkah lights themselves. The eight lights stand in a row; only the *shammash* may stand above them.

The order of lighting is as follows: On the first night the light at the right end of the lamp is lit. On the second night, and each night thereafter, another light is added to the left. The additional candle, marking the next day of Ḥanukkah, is always the first to be lit.

Liturgy

Two benedictions are recited before kindling the Ḥanukkah *Blessing the* lamp. The first is a blessing over the lights: "Blessed art Thou, O *Lights* Lord our God, King of the Universe, Who hast sanctified us by

Thy commandments, and commanded us to kindle the light of Hanukkah." The second blessing is for the miracle: "Blessed art Thou, O Lord our God, King of the Universe, Who wroughtest miracles for our fathers in days of old at this season."

On the first night the blessing of gratitude for the privilege of living to this moment *(she-heheyanu)* is added: "Blessed art Thou, O Lord our God, King of the Universe, Who hast kept us in life, and preserved us, and enabled us to reach this season."

The kindling of the lights is followed by a short reading *Ha-Nerot* which begins with the words *ha-nerot hallalu,* "these lights," and *Hallalu* lists the rules governing one's conduct during the times that the lights are burning.

By popular custom, the ceremony of kindling the Ḥanukkah *Ma'oz Ẓur* lights concludes with the singing of a hymn whose opening words are *ma'oz ẓur yeshu'ati,* "O Fortress, Rock of my salvation."

Ma—oz ẓur ye—shu—a—ti le-kha na—eh le-shab-be————ah
tik—kon bet te—fil—la—ti ve-sham to—dah ne-zab-be————ah le—
—et ta-khin mat-be————ah miz—ẓar ham-nab—be————ah
az eg—mor be—shir miz-mor ḥa-nuk—kat ham-miz—be————ah

The words were written in Germany, probably in the 13th century, by an author whose name was Mordecai. An acrostic spelling his name is formed from the first letter of each stanza. The first stanza expresses Israel's messianic hopes for the reestablishment of the ancient Temple worship. The following three stanzas praise God for the deliverance of Israel from the Egyptian

47

bondage, from the Babylonian exile, and from Haman's plot (see page 72). The fifth stanza summarizes the miracle of Ḥanukkah. A sixth stanza, which is said to refer to the German Emperor Frederic Barbarossa (12th century) is rarely sung.

A special prayer, *Al ha-Nissim* ("For the miracles") is recited on each of the eight days of the holiday during the *Amidah* and the grace after meals. *Al ha-Nissim*

The prayer gives thanks to God for the miracle of deliverance. It also stresses that heroism is not always to be found among the many in numbers, but in the few who are mighty.

Psalms 113—118 which express thanksgiving and joy for divine redemption, and which constitute the liturgical recitation known as *Hallel,* are also recited on each of the eight days of Ḥanukkah. *Hallel*

As is true of every Sabbath and each Jewish holiday, special readings from the Torah and the Prophets have been traditionally assigned to Ḥanukkah. Since Ḥanukkah itself is not mentioned in the Torah, the reading chosen was one describing the dedication of the sanctuary built while the Israelites wandered in the wilderness. This portion is read progressively on each morning of the holiday. *Torah Reading*

The search for an associated idea in the Prophets led to establishing the reading from Zechariah for the first Sabbath of Ḥanukkah. When a second Sabbath falls within the holiday week, a portion from the First Book of Kings is read. The first *haftarah* deals with Zechariah's vision of a gold *menorah,* symbolizing the restoration of the Jewish state, and includes the pertinent verse, "Not by might, nor by power, but by My spirit, saith the Lord of hosts." The second *Haftarah* describes the vessels, including the *menorot,* made for King Solomon's Temple.

In Sephardi communities, and in many Israeli synagogues, Psalm 30, "A song at the dedication of the House of David," is read on Ḥanukkah. It is considered likely that this psalm was sung at the rededication of the Temple by the Hasmoneans.

48

Custom

The Jew's sense of responsibility for his fellow Jew has always come to the fore at holiday-times. The poor among the community have to be cared for, and enabled to celebrate along with those who are more fortunate. When Jews lived in self-contained communities the poor would make the round of the wealthier Jewish households, which were expected to make suitable contributions for the purchase of holiday needs.

During the Middle Ages Maimonides wrote: "Even he who draws his sustenance from charity should borrow, or sell his cloak, to purchase oil and lamps (and kindle the Ḥanukkah lights)."

Gifts Ḥanukkah has also been the time for giving presents to teachers. It is even probable that their chief income, in centuries past, was derived from the Ḥanukkah gifts they received. The holiday was also marked by the exchange of gifts between the father of a betrothed maiden and her future bridegroom.

Children receive small sums of money, known in Europe as "Ḥanukkah gelt." This may also take the form of gold-wrapped chocolate coins.

Relating Miracles Ḥanukkah is a time of family gatherings, when "meals are to be punctuated with jest and song and the relating of miracles." In

The Chief Rabbi of Rumania, Dr. Moshe Rosen, distributes Ḥanukkah *gelt* to students of a Talmud Torah, 1950s.

49

ancient times one of the tales told at Ḥanukkah undoubtedly was that of the Hasmonean victory over the Syrian general Nicanor in 161 b.c.e. This victory was sufficiently important to have been celebrated by a feast marking the day of its occurrence. The thirteenth of Adar, and "Nicanor Day" is listed in *Megillat Ta'anit* (late first or early second centuries) as one of the "good days" established during the period of the Second Temple. This feast day was still observed among the Jews of Palestine in the 7th and 9th centuries, but has since disappeared from the Jewish calendar. Ironically, the thirteenth of Adar is now marked by a fast, not a feast (see page 70).

Foods

Jews of all communities eat pastry and potato preparations fried in oil, as a reminder of the miracle of the jar of oil at the rededication of the Temple. Ashkenazim call them *latkes,* or *fasputshes,* or *pontshkes.* They are also called *zalaviyye* (Yemen), *dushpire* (Bukhara), *ata-if* (Iraq), *spanzes* (Tripoli), and by Sephardim in general *birmenailes.* In Israel *sufganiyyot* (doughnuts), and *levivot* (potato pancakes) are traditional Ḥanukkah fare.

Illustration from an Armenian Bible, showing Judith with the head of Holofernes. Constantinople, mid-17th century.

Documents from the 14th century indicate that the custom of eating cheese pancakes was already in existence. This custom is connected with the story of Judith (see page 57), who is said to have fed Holofernes cheese to make him thirsty and encourage him to drink more wine.

50

18th century engraving of a Ḥanukkah celebration, with children playing games and adults gambling (above). A 19th century ivory *dreidl* from Russia (right).

Jews in Eastern Europe eat *retekh salat* at Ḥanukkah. It is made of radish, turnip, olives, and onions fried in goose fat with *gribenes* (cracklings) — ingredients held to have been popular in the Maccabean era. Yemenite Jews eat *laḥis gizar,* a sort of carrot stew, at this season.

Participation in games, generally frowned upon in Jewish communities as a waste of time that should be devoted to the study of the Torah, was permitted during the week of Ḥanukkah.

Games

The most popular game, especially with children, was *dreidl* or *trendl* (a top; in modern Hebrew — *sevivon*). The game provides an excellent example of how a foreign custom was ingeniously Judaized.

The idea of the *dreidl,* a four-sided top which is spun in a gambling game during Ḥanukkah, was probably borrowed from a

51

three-sided top spun by German Christians on Christmas eve. The Ḥanukkah *dreidl* traditionally bears four Hebrew letters on its sides: *nun, gimel, heh, shin*. These are interpreted as the initial letters of the words of a Hebrew phrase: *nes gadol haya sham*, "a great miracle took place there." Actually they were borrowed from the four letters inscribed on dice used in Germany in the Middle Ages. These letters, *n, g, h, s*, were the initials of four words which decided the result of the wager on the dice: *nichts* (nothing), *ganz* (all), *halb* (half) and *shtell ein* (put in). In modern Israel the letters on the *sevivon* are *nun, gimel, heh, peh*, standing for *nes gadol haya po*, "a great miracle took place *here*."

Ḥanukkah is also the only time in the year when Judaism looks upon gambling with a sympathetic eye. Even children may be found betting on the turn of the *dreidl*, using nuts or Ḥanukkah *gelt* as their stakes.

In addition to *dreidl* games, card-playing is an acceptable diversion at Ḥanukkah (in Sephardi communities at Purim). Card games made their appearance in the 15th century, and soon gained a popular following. Many Jewish communities enacted rules forbidding the fascinating game, but almost always Ḥanukkah was mentioned as a time when card-playing was permitted. Some communities produced special "Jewish cards", inscribed with Hebrew letters and illustrated with pictures of figures from Jewish history and folklore.

During the Middle Ages it was customary to read the "Scroll of Antiochus" in the synagogue on Ḥanukkah. This scroll is a popular – partly historical, partly fictional – account of the events surrounding the holiday. It was handed down in several Aramaic versions, probably dating from the late talmudic period (5th and 6th centuries c.e.), and was then translated into Hebrew and into various languages which the Jews spoke in different countries.

It is apparent that the author of the "Scroll of Antiochus" was ignorant of the historical circumstances at the time of the

Scroll of Antiochus

Maccabees. However, the work does reflect the customs and recollections which the people of his time cherished regarding the Hasmonean victory.

The custom of reading this scroll during Ḥanukkah has been abandoned.

The Menorah

The main ritual of the eight-day Ḥanukkah festival is the kindling of the lights in the *menorah* (in modern Hebrew, *ḥanukkiyyah;* plural, *menorot, ḥanukkiyyot*). Two definite types of *menorot* can be distinguished: (1) the "bench type" which is usually small, has a back wall, and is often richly ornamented; (2) the standing form which developed during the Middle Ages, and is reminiscent of the *menorah* which stood in the Temple, with the difference that it has nine branches (eight plus the *shammash*), whereas the Temple *menorah* had seven branches. Tradition prohibits the exact duplication of this *menorah*.

The richly decorated Ḥanukkah lamp had its origin in the *Ancient Lamps* simple pear-shaped, clay oil lamp with a small opening for the wick and a larger one for the oil, that was in use throughout the Mediterranean world during the Roman period. These lamps were mounted on bases for Ḥanukkah use, and were modified to accommodate eight wicks, fed by a central oil reservoir. Similar lamps were used until recently by the Jews of Yemen and Persia.

During the period of the Mishnah, when it was customary to place the Ḥanukkah lamp outside the entrance of the house, it was inserted into "a glass lantern," to prevent the lights from being extinguished by the wind.

Metal lamps came into use in the talmudic period, and were *Metal Menorot* generally adopted for use on Ḥanukkah. Despite the regulation stating that the Ḥanukkah lamp was to be placed outside the door, or at the window, at an early period it became the rule to light the Ḥanukkah lamp within the home. In many situations and at many times, "proclaiming the miracle" also meant pro-

53

claiming the fact that one was a Jew; this was to invite trouble, and even death. By the eighth century the great sages known as *geonim* felt it necessary to permit Jews to ignore this rule, and to light the Ḥanukkah lamp within their homes.

This change in custom was reflected in the changing form of the *menorah*. Since it no longer stood outside the home or near the doorway, but was lit indoors, a back-wall was added, with a hook for hanging purposes. This type of lamp originated in Spain and from there spread to other countries; similar lamps are found in Morocco, Italy, France and Poland.

Until recently, Sephardi communities throughout the world maintained the custom of hanging the *menorah* near the door. Ḥanukkah lamps from Spanish Morocco are often inscribed with the verse: "Blessed are you at your coming and blessed are you at your leaving." North African Jewry made their *menorot* of stone and glazed pottery, or of engraved hammered-brass. In Iraq and Persia the traditional Ḥanukkah lamps were made of stone or metal, and were round.

During the Renaissance in Italy, the *menorah* reached new *Ornamental* heights of ornamentation, in the style of the period. It was *Menorot* generally cast in copper, bronze or brass, and was decorated with cherubs, masks and cornucopiae, with figures from biblical stories and even with the coats of arms of noble patrons.

In Eastern Europe legs were often added to the back-wall of the *menorah*, as it was the custom to stand the lamp on the windowsill or on a table. These lamps were frequently worked in filigree and decorated with Torah crowns, lions, eagles and other such figures.

It is related that Rabbi Meir of Rothenberg (Germany) *Synagogue* kindled the Ḥanukkah lights in "small metal vessels," most likely *Menorot* adding another vessel each night.

Along with the great variety of *menorot* crafted for home use, large standing *menorot* are made for synagogue use. In the synagogue the Ḥanukkah *menorah* is to be placed on the southern

Ḥanukkiyyot (clockwise from top left): Silver filigree from Galacia, 18th century; Brass from Spanish Morocco, 17th century; Silver, Israel, 20th century; Painted ceramic from Libya, 19th century; Brass from Poland, 17th century.

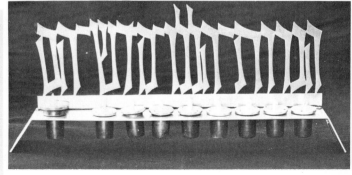

wall, corresponding to the location of the golden *menorah* in the Temple. Early examples of these *menorot* are rare, as they were frequently confiscated during wars, to be melted down and their metal cast into weapons.

Since the 18th century, the standing *menorah* has also been adapted for the use of candles in the home.

Contemporary artists have sought to combine traditional Jewish motifs with elements of modern art and new techniques, and have further modified the design of the *menorah*. *Modern Menorot*

In Music and Art

In addition to the opportunities to express craftsmanship and artistic flair provided by the *menorah*, the themes and figures associated with Ḥanukkah have frequently been represented in music and in the arts.

Perhaps the best-known musical work associated with the holiday is Handel's outstanding oratorio, *Judas Maccabeus*, first performed in 1747.

The treasury of world culture has also been enriched by works of art and music based on the stories of two women — Hannah and Judith — who displayed unusual valor in defending the Jewish faith and the Jewish people, and whose names are traditionally associated with the holiday of Ḥanukkah.

Chapter 7 of the Second Book of Maccabees relates the story of seven brothers who were seized along with their mother by Antiochus Epiphanes, shortly after the beginning of his religious persecutions. The brothers were commanded to eat the flesh of a pig. They defiantly refused to do so and, despite the threat of death, were encouraged in their stand by their mother. As a result, one by one, beginning with the eldest, each was tortured horribly and then executed before his mother's eyes. When only the youngest son remained, the king appealed to the mother to tell the child to eat the forbidden meat, so that his life might be spared. The mother refused to do so, and stoically *Hannah*

56

Kindling the Ḥanukkah lights at the Western Wall, Jerusalem, 1972. Every evening at sundown during Ḥanukkah, the lights are kindled by a public figure.

Scouts taking part in the ceremonial kindling of the Ḥanukkah torch at Modi'in. The torch is relayed by runners from the site of the Maccabean tombs to Jerusalem.

"The Purim Players", a tempera painting by Joseph Herman, c. 1942, London.

Megillah, Morocco, early 19th century. The decorative panels give the genealogy of Mordecai and Haman, tracing the former through Jacob to Abraham and the latter only as far as Esau.

watched her last child killed. She herself died shortly thereafter.

This story is also told in great emotional detail in the Fourth Book of Maccabees, dating from the first century c.e.

The accounts of the manner in which the mother met her death differ. One says that she threw herself into the fire on the defiled altar. Another has it that she jumped to her death from a roof. According to yet another version, she fell dead of grief on the corpses of her children.

Although the name of the mother is not given in the Second Book of Maccabees, she is called Miriam in various rabbinic retellings of the tragic story. However, in 16th century Spain, a scholar who was revising Jewish sources named the mother "Hannah" (because of the verse in the First Book of Samuel, " . . . while the barren has borne seven, she that had many children has languished," which was part of Hannah's prayer). By that name the courageous Jewish mother has become famous.

The Book of Judith probably dates from the Hasmonean *Judith* period, and is included by Jews in the Apocrypha (see page 36). It is generally held to be fiction, based on historical events which took place in 352 b.c.e., when a Cappadocian (Asia Minor) prince named Holofernes fought against the Egyptians. Undoubtedly it was written to inspire courage among the small group of Hasmonean supporters in their rebellion against the Seleucid Greeks.

The story is as follows: Nebuchadnezzar, king of Assyria, sent Holofernes, his commander-in-chief, on a campaign of conquest in the Near East. When Holofernes reached the valley of Esdraelon and the narrow mountain pass leading to Judea and Jerusalem, he found that, by order of the High Priest in Jerusalem, it had been occupied by the Jews living in the forti-fied towns of the region. Holofernes then laid siege to one of the towns, Bethulia. After a month, when the town's water supply had been depleted, its leaders decided to open the gates to the enemy. Then a young, beautiful and righteous widow named

57

58

Judith, the daughter of Merari of the tribe of Simeon, appeared before them. With the permission of the leaders of the town, Judith went down to the camp of Holofernes. The general, attracted by her beauty and wisdom, invited her to a feast. Judith encouraged Holofernes to drink much wine, until he fell into a drunken stupor. While he slept, she took his dagger, and cut off his head. Deprived of their commander-in-chief by Judith's courageous deed, the Assyrian soldiers fled.

Although the book has come down to us in various Greek, Aramaic, and Latin versions, it is clear from the character of the language that these were translations from an original Hebrew text.

The story of Judith has frequently been used as a theme by musicians, artists and writers. Judith was a popular figure in the art of medieval Christians who saw her as the symbol of the triumph of the Virgin over the devil. In the 16th century the story of Judith aroused new attention among Protestant writers who interpreted it as the triumph of virtue over wickedness. Martin Luther, who favored biblical subjects for drama, recommended the use of the story of Judith as a tragic theme.

Since the mid-19th-century, when biblical subjects became an acceptable theme for public secular performances, and when audiences had grown sufficiently "sophisticated" to be shown Holofernes' severed head on the stage, operas about Judith have multiplied.

In the Twentieth Century

The festival of Ḥanukkah has assumed new meaning for contemporary Jews, who recognize in it the first serious attempt by a minority group to maintain its religious and cultural individuality within the framework of the larger society. Judah Maccabee and his brothers fought not for the right of the Jews to be like everyone else, but for their right to be different.

In this sense, the holiday speaks directly to Jews — but at the

59

"Judith and Holofernes," bronze sculpture by Donatello, 1455-7. It stands in the Piazza della Signoria, Florence.

same time it has much more than purely Jewish significance, for it proclaims the right of every minority group to assert and defend its own unique values against the pressures of conformity to the majority culture.

Ḥanukkah also teaches that the only effective answer to oppression is to take a positive stand on those values which oppression threatens to wipe out. The Hasmoneans not only fought *against* Antiochus and his hellenizing decrees; they also fought *for* Judaism. Their victory was marked by the cleansing of the Temple and the rededication of its altar to God.

Ḥanukkah has gained added importance in Jewish life since the development of modern Jewish nationalism. Its themes of the preservation of the minority's values, and the victory of the small band of stubbornly courageous Jews over a mighty empire, spoke to the hearts of the determined Zionists who were fighting the British mandatory power and world opinion in their effort to express the spirit of Jewish national renaissance in a Jewish homeland. Because of its "relevance," the observance of the holiday of Ḥanukkah spread to secular Jewish circles in which other religious festivals were minimized or ignored. *Zionism*

An often-told episode of the Hasmonean revolt also struck a responsive chord among the early settlers of Palestine, who frequently saw themselves as modern Maccabees. It is told that a group of Hasmonean refugees was attacked by Greek soldiers on the Sabbath. Refusing to defend themselves on the day of rest, the group, numbering about 1,000, was almost totally wiped out. This led Mattathias, the High Priest, to decree that defensive military action was permissible on the Sabbath.

In Israel, giant *menorot,* are lit on the roofs of public build-ings during Ḥanukkah. Among the most distinctive are the *menorah* topping the Knesset (parliament) building in Jerusalem, and since 1967, the Ḥanukkah lamps lit at the Western Wall. *In Israel*

The eight days of Ḥanukkah are marked by parties, gala dinners, concerts and other festivities. Youth groups organize

60

torchlight parades, ending in a *kumsitz*, an informal gathering around a campfire.

In recent years Israelis have begun to make pilgrimages to Modi'in, the city in which the Hasmonean revolt broke out. Modi'in has been identified by archaeologists with a village just east of Lydda, Israel's international airport, on the ancient road to Jerusalem. The tombs of the Maccabees have been tentatively located across the valley from the village.

The Hanukkah torch starts out from Modi'in (above). Runner in the relay from Modi'in to Jerusalem (top right). The Chief Rabbi of Israel, Rabbi Unterman, lighting the first candle of Hanukkah at the Western Wall, 1968 (right).

On the first evening of Ḥanukkah a torch is solemnly lit at the tombs and raced, in relays, to Jerusalem, where it is used to kindle the large *menorah* at the presidential residence.

In the United States, Ḥanukkah has assumed great importance as a family and gift-giving holiday. An attempt is made to provide Jewish children with a celebration that will *In the United States* offset the all-pervading Christmas spirit of the society around them. In addition to candlelighting, gifts are exchanged among the members of the family. Often children are given small gifts on each of the eight nights, after the candles are lit.

The significance of Ḥanukkah, its ability to speak to many successive generations of Jews, was beautifully summed up by Louis D. Brandeis, justice of the United States Supreme Court, and a loyal and active supporter of the Zionist movement. Brandeis saw in Ḥanukkah a message of meaning and inspiration for all Americans: *Louis D. Brandeis*

> Ḥanukkah, the Feast of the Maccabees, celebrates a victory — not a military victory only, but a victory also of the spirit over things material. Not a victory only over external enemies — the Greeks; but a victory also over more dangerous internal enemies. A victory of the many over the ease-loving, safety-playing, privileged, powerful few, who in their pliancy would have betrayed the best interests of the people, a victory of democracy over aristocracy.

> As part of the eternal world-wide struggle for democracy, the struggle of the Maccabees is of eternal world-wide interest. It is a struggle of the Jews of today as well as of those of two thousand years ago. It is a struggle in which all Americans, non-Jews as well as Jews, should be vitally interested because they are vitally affected.

6.　TU BI-SHEVAT

Tu bi-Shevat literally means "the fifteenth day of the month of Shevat" (see page 31). That day, which generally falls within the months of January-February, marks the "New Year of Trees" in the Jewish tradition.

62

Four New Years

The Jewish calendar is unique in having four separate days each known as a "New Year". They are listed in the Mishnah, where they are explained as having civil, political, religious and agricultural significance.

The first of Nisan (late March or early April) is the New Year for (Jewish) kings and for festivals. Thus, if a king ascended the throne during Adar, the following month, Nisan, would be considered the beginning of the second year of his reign. Passover, which falls on the fifteenth of Nisan, is considered to be the first festival of the year. The Talmud also lists other activities which are governed by this New Year.

The first of Elul (August — early September) is the New Year for the tithing of cattle. That is, the tithes of cattle brought each year to the priests in the Temple were computed on cattle born from the first of Elul until the thirtieth of Av.

The first of Tishrei (September—October) is the New Year for the civil calendar, and for the counting of the reigns of foreign kings. It also marked the beginning of the Sabbatical and Jubilee years, and of the year for planting fruit and vegetables. The first of Tishrei is considered the religious New Year as well, since Rosh Ha-Shanah falls on that date. The Talmud holds that on that day "all the world is judged."

The first of Shevat (January) is the New Year for Trees according to the School of Shammai; but the School of Hillel fixed the date as the fifteenth of Shevat (mid January—February).

Hillel's date for the New Year for Trees, the fifteenth of Shevat, has been accepted as the norm in Judaism. The Talmud explains the decision in terms of rainfall; the greater part of the year's rain in the Land of Israel having fallen by the fifteenth of Shevat. In Israel, the winter is the rainy season; the summer is the dry season. Another talmudic explanation for the decision is that the winter season with its heavy rainfall comes to an end on this

A Scholarly Argument

63

day, and the sap of the trees becomes active, bringing new life to the trees. Consequently, for purposes of levying tithes and for other religious-agricultural purposes, the fruits of those trees which blossom after the fifteenth of Shevat are considered to belong to the new year.

A ninth century sage, Rav Hai Gaon, related Hillel's ruling to an Arab tradition that in the month of Shevat, God throws down three burning coals to warm the earth. On the seventh of Shevat the first coal falls, to warm the air. On the fourteenth of Shevat the second coal falls to heat the water which begins to enter the trees. On the twenty-first of the month the third coal is thrown, to warm the soil. It is on the fourteenth of Shevat that the Arabs say, "Today water has entered the trees," marking the New Year of Trees.

Modern scholars have suggested that the difference in the viewpoints of Hillel and Shammai may be explained by geographic and climatic factors. The followers of Hillel lived, in general, in Jerusalem and the Judean hills, whereas the followers of Shammai were large landowners whose agricultural holdings were in the plains. Trees generally bud at Jerusalem's high altitude about two weeks later than in the lowlands, so that the Hillelites fixed the New Year for Trees at a later date.

Customs

The New Year for Trees is regarded as a minor or semi-holiday. *Liturgy* Accordingly, no penitential prayers are said during the services, and fasting is not permitted. Otherwise, there is no special liturgy marking the day.

The Sephardi Jews invested the New Year for Trees with *Sephardi* great significance. Under the influence of the kabbalists of 16th *Influence* century Safed, the characteristic Sephardi liturgy and customs for this festival were developed. From Safed they spread to Sephardi communities in Turkey, Italy, and Greece, and then to other parts of Europe, Asia and North Africa.

Among Sephardim the day is known as The Feast of Fruits, and special poems, called *complas,* are recited. A home service is held around the table, and blessings are pronounced over wheat, barley, grapes, figs, pomegranates, olives, and honey, the "seven species" with which the Land of Israel was blessed. Charity distributed on that day is known as *ma'ot perot,* "fruit money" (just as charity distributed for Passover is known as *ma'ot hittim,* "wheat money"), and children are presented with a *bolsa de frutas,* a "bag of fruit" at a Tu bi-Shevat party.

On the eve of Tu bi-Shevat the Sephardim of Jerusalem arrange special parties in the synagogues and *yeshivot,* which last through the night. Portions from the Torah, Mishnah, Talmud and Zohar are read, each containing references to the agricultural life of the Land of Israel. These selections appear in a special booklet called *Peri Ez Hadar,* "The Goodly Fruit".

16th-century collections of religious customs practiced in various Jewish communities note that the Jews in Erez Israel and the adjoining countries were in the habit of eating fruit on Tu bi-Shevat, and reciting special hymns and songs in the synagogue.

During the days of the great kabbalist, Isaac ben Solomon Luria (1534—1572), known from the initials of his title and name (*Ha-Elohi Rabbi Yizhak,* "the divine rabbi") as "Ha-Ari", the kabbalists of Safed developed new forms and rituals for the New Year for Trees. Lovers of nature, they would go out into the fields to observe the changes of the seasons. In a ritual symbolizing the varying colors of the land at that time of the year, they drank four cups of wine: the first was of white wine; the second was white wine mixed with a little red wine; the third — of red wine mixed with a little white wine; the fourth - entirely of red wine.

Later, the drinking of the four cups of wine was part of a special ritual practiced on the fifteenth of Shevat, a service modeled on the Passover *seder.* The ritual bore the name *Hemdat ha-Yamim,* and is believed to have been compiled by

Nathan of Gaza, a 17th century Palestinian mystic who was a leading figure in the messianic movement led by Shabbetai Zevi. The meal which accompanied the service would consist of no less than fifteen (for the fifteenth of Shevat) types of fruit and, like the Passover *seder*, would include four cups of wine.

The fruits of Tu bi-Shevat; a woodcut from from an early 18th century book of customs, Amsterdam.

In communities of more northern latitudes in Europe, fresh fruits were difficult to come by in mid-winter. Yet the custom of eating fruit on Tu bi-Shevat prevailed, and special emphasis was placed on the fruits which grew in the Land of Israel. Jewish communities in Eastern Europe would enjoy dried fruits such as dates, figs, raisins and almonds and, when available, an expensive orange.

A fruit of the Holy Land that appears in Jewish homes throughout the world on Tu bi-Shevat (and generally only then)

In Ashkenazi Communities

66

is the carob (*bokser* in Yiddish). It is also known as St. John's Bread, for scholars have suggested that John the Baptist ate carobs when he went into the wilderness preaching repentance. (The traditional narrative has him eating locusts, but the Greek word for locusts may also be translated as carobs.)

The eating of fruits is accompanied by the recitation of Psalm 104 which describes God's greatness as manifested in nature, and of the 15 "Songs of Ascents" (Psalms 120—134).

Ḥasidim have a tradition that Tu bi-Shevat is the day on which the fate of trees and fruits is decided. Accordingly, on that day they pray that the *etrogim,* the citron fruit, may grow in beauty and perfection in order to be enjoyed on the holiday of Sukkot.

Ties with the Land

During the long period of Diaspora living, Tu bi-Shevat provided an emotional link between Jews and the Land of Israel. A religious poem written by Rabbi Yehuda ben Rabbi Hillel in the 10th century, and found in the Cairo *genizah* (a great storeroom of old books and manuscripts which was brought to light in the late 19th century), expresses the plaintive emotions of a Jew who celebrates the New Year for Trees when he himself is unable to fulfill the commandment of settling in the Holy Land and complying with the agricultural laws set down in the Bible.

There is no doubt that the practice of eating fruits that grow in the Holy Land was an important factor in keeping the ties between the Jewish people and the Holy Land alive and flourishing throughout the generations.

With the return of Jewish colonizers to Palestine at the turn *In Palestine* of the century, there was a need to create a more pragmatic expression of maintaining ties with the land, a practice that would not have to be limited to the symbolism inherent in eating the fruits of the land.

In the early decades of the 20th century, the teachers and

community leaders of the small Jewish population in Palestine made a concerted effort to inject new content into the holiday. Tu bi-Shevat acquired new significance, symbolizing the revival and redemption of the land by the conquest of the desert. New songs and dances were created in honor of the New Year for Trees. The flowering almond tree, one of the first fruit-bearing trees to blossom in late winter, became the symbol of the holiday.

An almond tree in bloom, symbolic of Tu-bi-Shevat (left). Tel Aviv kindergarden children preparing to plant saplings (below).

As part of the massive project of the Jewish National Fund to restore forests to the denuded and eroded hillsides of the land, the school-children would go out into the countryside on Tu bi-Shevat to plant tens of thousands of saplings. Communities in the Diaspora were also encouraged to participate in the broad program of afforestation and soil conservation by purchasing "Tree Certificates" on Tu bi-Shevat. This custom has been retained in Israel. Tree-planting stations have been set up in various parts of the country to enable foreign visitors to participate in this project as well.

Afforestation

Concern for Trees
Concern for the natural resources of Erez Israel, and for its trees

68

in particular, is not a new concept among Jews. The awareness of what we now call "ecological principles" was apparent even in biblical times.

Among the regulations which the Torah provides to govern the life of the Jews in the Land of Israel was one which stated:

> When in your war against a city you have to besiege it a long time in order to capture it, you must not destroy its trees, wielding the ax against them. You may eat of them, but you must not cut them down. Are trees of the field human, to withdraw before you under siege? Only trees which you know do not yield food may be destroyed; you may cut them down for constructing siege-works against the city that is waging war on you, until it has been reduced.

The concern for trees, and the awareness of their importance in the larger interrelationship of man and nature, is also evident in the teaching of the rabbis. In commenting on the biblical verse urging the planting of trees in the Land of Israel they said:

> The Holy One blessed-be-He said to Israel: Even though you will find the land filled with all that is good, you shall not say, "We will settle and not plant." Rather you shall hasten to plant. Just as you entered the land and found trees planted by others, you too shall plant for your children. Let no man say: "I am old; how much longer shall I live? Why should I labor for others who will enjoy the fruits of my work after I am dead?" Therefore, man should not refrain from planting, but rather he should add to the trees that he found planted before his lifetime, even if he is old.

Rabbi Johanan ben Zakkai said: "If you hold a sapling in your hand, ready to plant it, and you are told, 'The Messiah is here!' — first plant the sapling, and then go forth to welcome him."

Rabbinic concern for the world of nature was also expressed in this aphorism: "When one chops down a fruit-bearing tree, its cry goes forth from one end of the world to the other — but its cry is not heard."

Full Circle
The holiday of Tu bi-Shevat has come full circle in its observance and significance. From the New Year for Trees in biblical times, when the Jewish farmer would estimate the amount of his obligatory priestly contributions from the fruit of his trees, the day became a Day of Fruits in the Diaspora, expressing the yearning of exiled Jewish communities for the Land of Israel. Since the land has again been settled, the New Year for Trees has been restored to its full meaning; the trees of the land once again contribute to the welfare of the people living on the land.

7. PURIM

In the cycle of the Jewish year, Purim may be considered a "minor festival", but it occupies a major place in the hearts of the Jewish people. It is the most joyous and carefree of the Jewish holidays, and the lesson it teaches, that evil will be punished and that righteousness will prevail, has provided hope and a message of faith to Jews living under the most difficult conditions throughout the world. The rabbis of the Talmud declared that even when the Messiah appears and the other holidays will be abandoned, Purim will continue to be observed.

The Joy of Adar
Because of the festive nature of Purim, and because other days in the month of Adar commemorate such joyous occasions as the Hasmonean victory over the Syrian general Nicanor (see page 50), the day the order was given to rebuild the walls of Jerusalem

70

after its destruction, a miraculous escape of the sages from their enemies, etc. — the entire month has taken on a joyful character. This is expressed in a talmudic aphorism: "When Adar begins, joy is increased."

The Scroll of Esther
Purim (the Feast of Lots), which falls on the fourteenth of Adar (generally in March), commemorates the triumph of Esther and Mordecai over the wicked Haman who sought to exterminate all the Jews of the Persian Empire. The events are related in the Scroll of Esther, known in Hebrew as *Megillat Ester* (*megillah* = scroll).

This is the story told by the *Megillah:* The Persian king, Ahasuerus, in the third year of his reign, climaxed 180 days of banqueting with his officials by an additional feast of seven days

The beginning of an illuminated Esther Scroll, Italy or Holland, 17-18th century.

for the entire populace of Shushan, the capital city. On the seventh day of this party the drunken king ordered Queen Vashti to appear so that all would appreciate her beauty. When the queen refused, the king, after consulting with his advisers, removed Vashti from her position.

A contest was then held among all the beautiful maidens of the kingdom to seek a new queen. One of the girls taken to the palace was Esther, or Hadassah, a Jewish orphan who had been brought up by her cousin Mordecai. Esther concealed her Jewish origins, and because of her beauty and charm was chosen by the king to succeed Vashti.

Mordecai, one of the officials who "sat in the King's gate", overheard a plot against the king. He revealed it to Esther, who in turn informed the king. The conspirators were executed, and Mordecai's name was recorded in the king's Book of Chronicles.

King Ahasuerus elevated Haman above his other courtiers and all the king's courtiers bowed down to him in recognition of his distinguished rank. When Mordecai refused to do so, Haman resolved to exterminate Mordecai and the entire Jewish people. He determined the appropriate day for their destruction by lot (pur; therefore the name Purim). In order to carry out his intention, Haman persuaded the king that the Jews were a subversive people, and reinforced his argument with an offer of 10,000 talents of silver. The king authorized Haman to deal with the Jews as he wished. Haman wrote to all the royal governors and informed them that on the thirteenth of Adar all the Jews in their regions were to be slaughtered.

Mordecai learned of the decree and appealed to Esther to intercede with Ahasuerus. In spite of the mortal danger of appearing before the king without a specific summons, Esther said that she would fast three days and then go to him. On the third day, she approached King Ahasuerus, who received her graciously. She requested that the king and Haman come to a banquet that same day. There she did not reveal her intention, but

Part of the *Adloyada* carnival
procession in Tel Aviv, 1968.

Tanks in formation passing the Old City walls during Israel's 25th anniversary parade.

Dancing and merrymaking in Jerusalem's Zion Square on the eve of Israel's 25th Independence Day, 1973.

merely asked Ahasuerus and Haman to attend a second banquet that she would prepare for the following day. Haman returned home proud of being so honored. Upon the advice of his wife and supporters, he prepared a gallows 50 cubits high, upon which to hang Mordecai.

Since the king could not sleep that night, he ordered that the Book of Chronicles be read to him. When he discovered that Mordecai had never been rewarded for reporting the conspiracy against the king, he asked Haman's advice concerning a means of rewarding someone whom the king deemed worthy of honor. Haman believed that he was the chosen one and proposed that the man to be honored be dressed in royal clothing, seated on the king's horse and led through the streets of the city. A noble was to lead the horse and proclaim: "This is what is done for the man whom the king desires to honor." The king then ordered Haman to do this for Mordecai.

Later that day, during the second banquet, Queen Esther revealed her Jewish origin to the king, begged for her life and the life of her people, and revealed that an enemy was plotting the destruction of the Jews — Haman. In anger, Ahasuerus strode into the palace garden, and Haman fell on Esther's couch to plead for his life. The king returned to find Haman in this compromising position, and gave orders for him to be hanged on the gallows prepared for Mordecai.

Haman's place in the king's favor was taken over by Mordecai who wrote to all the royal governors in the realm, authorizing the Jews to defend themselves. Thus, instead of being exterminated on the thirteenth of Adar, the Jews killed their enemies. At Esther's request, the Jews of the capital, Shushan, were also given the following day, the fourteenth of Adar, to avenge themselves.

The days following the battles, the fourteenth of Adar in the provinces, and the fifteenth in Shushan, were declared by Mordecai and Esther as days of feasting and rejoicing forever, and were called "days of Purim" to commemorate the lots that Haman cast.

Entry into Jewish Calendar

The first mention of Purim in Jewish literature occurs in the first century b.c.e., when the Second Book of Maccabees mentions the "Day of Mordecai" that was celebrated on the fourteenth of Adar.

Haman leading Mordecai on the King's horse; painted by Rembrandt, 1606.

It would seem that although the rabbis agreed that the Scroll of Esther was divinely inspired, there was considerable hesitation on their part to grant it official recognition as a holy book and accept it into the canon of the Bible. The arguments presented for and against the decision are recorded in Tractate Megillah of the Talmud. In the end, the rabbis did accept the Scroll of Esther as one of Judaism's sacred works, and it is included in the third section of the Holy Scriptures.

The Scroll of Esther is unique among the books of the Bible in that the name of God does not appear in it. Nonetheless, the intervention of the hand of Providence may be discerned repeatedly behind the exploits of the main figures in the story.

It is clear that some time before the destruction of the Second Temple (70 c.e.) the Scroll of Esther had achieved a sufficient degree of official recognition for its reading to be obligatory on the fourteenth of Adar. The Talmud records that the priests officiating at the Temple service were required to leave their duties to listen to the reading of the *Megillah*.

Because the Jews of the capital city of Shushan, which was *Shushan Purim* encircled by a wall, did not celebrate Purim on the fourteenth of Adar as did those in the provinces, but rather marked the day on the fifteenth, it is customary that Jews living in towns that are considered to have been walled in the days of Joshua fulfill the laws of Purim on the fifteenth of the month. That day is called *Shushan Purim*.

Thus, the city of Jerusalem marks the holiday on the fifteenth of Adar, and anyone in Israel who wishes to enjoy two Purims a year can celebrate on the fourteenth, and then once again on the fifteenth in Jerusalem.

A rare occurrence is the fifteenth of Adar falling on a Sabbath in which case inhabitants of "walled" cities need not leave their homes in order to enjoy three successive days of Purim. In order to avoid a desecration of the Sabbath the mitzvot (see page 79) of the festival are re-arranged as follows: the *Megillah* is read on

Thursday night and Friday morning as though the city were not "walled" and gifts are given to the poor prior to the Sabbath; the *Al ha-Nissim* prayer as well as the special section from the Torah are read on the Sabbath, *mishlo'ah manot* and the festive meal take place on Sunday.

In a leap year, an extra month is added to the Jewish calendar *Purim Katan* (see page 4), and that month is generally known as "Second Adar" *(Adar Sheni);* the original month is called the "First Adar" *(Adar Rishon).* In a leap year, Purim is celebrated during the second month of Adar, and the fourteenth and fifteenth days of the first Adar are known as *Purim katan,* the "minor Purim". According to the talmudic tradition, Purim should be celebrated in Second Adar because the original Purim occurred in the Second Adar of a leap year.

Purim katan is not governed by the rituals of Purim (see page 79). The *Megillah* is not read, and no gifts are sent to the poor. It is, however, a minor festival, and therefore the *Taḥanun* prayer is not recited.

History and Folklore

Is the story related in the Scroll of Esther historical truth, or romantic fiction? In favor of a historical interpretation is the accurate description of Persian customs and court practices recorded by the author, who is thought to have been a Persian Jew. King Ahasuerus is generally identified as Xerxes I of Persia (485–465 b.c.e.), although it has also been suggested that the events took place during the reign of Artaxerxes (403–358 b.c.e.). In a tablet found at an archaeological site in Persia, mention is made of a royal official named Marduka who lived around the time of Xerxes I.

However, no reference has yet been found in any Persian document to a king who had a Jewish wife. Indeed, it is known that the Persian kings were permitted to choose their wives only from among seven noble families, which would preclude choosing

76

Silver cases for the Scroll of Esther. From left to right: Italy,
17th century; Italy c. 19th century; Salonica, 19th century.

77

a wife as Ahasuerus did Esther.

Some scholars consider the Book of Esther to be a narrative set in Persia for dramatic purposes, but actually referring to events that took place during the time of the Maccabees (second century b.c.e.) or of King Herod (first century b.c.e.).

Another critical school of thought points to the striking similarity of the names of Mordecai and Esther and those of the Babylonian gods, Marduk and Ishtar. These scholars suggest that the story may be derived from an account of the conflicts of

Contemporary *megillah;* the olive wood case is covered with depictions of the holy places.

these gods or of their worshippers. In ancient Persia a festival known as Farvardigan, which marked the end of winter, was celebrated on the fourteenth day of the twelfth month of the year and, like Purim, was characterized by much gaiety and with the exchange of gifts.

Recent literary research suggests that while the Book of

Esther may ultimately be based on actual events, it contains two independent plots derived from oriental romances. One is a plot of harem intrigue, of which Esther is the heroine; the other is a tale of court intrigue, of which Mordecai is the hero.

Whatever its origin, Purim has assumed a respected place in Jewish literature and practices. The kabbalists, Jewish mystics of the 16th century, regarded Purim so highly that they said, punningly, that the Day of Atonement (Hebrew: *Yom Kippurim*) is "a day like Purim" *(yom ke-Purim)*. In ḥasidic literature much is made of Purim as a day of friendship and joy, and a day which celebrates the working of God "behind the scenes." The "lots" of Purim were compared with the "lots" cast on the Day of Atonement, and the lesson derived from them is that what human beings call "fate" or "luck" is really only another manifestation of God's care.

The Five Mitzvot

Five *mitzvot* are associated with the celebration of Purim: reading the *Megillah;* reading a portion of the Torah; sending gifts to friends and relatives; distribution of charity to the poor; and participation in a festive meal, known as the Purim *se'udah*.

Laws of the Megillah

The first duty to be fulfilled on Purim, as legislated in the Talmud, is the public reading of the *Megillah* on the fourteenth of Adar. An additional reading is to take place on the eve of the holiday. Although women are exempt from those positive duties of Jewish Law that are to be fulfilled at a fixed time, they are required to be present at the *Megillah* reading, since the feast celebrates the deliverance of the Jews through the intervention of a woman.

The story of Purim must be read (not recited from memory) *Preparation of* from a scroll (not a book). The scroll must be handwritten on *the Scroll* vellum (the skin of a lamb, kid or calf) or parchment (the skin of a sheep or goat), according to the stringent regulations which govern the preparation of a Torah scroll or of any part of the Bible destined for liturgical use.

Because the word "the king" appears so frequently in the *Megillah*, the rabbis have suggested that whenever it appears without the name Ahasuerus next to it, it refers to the King of the Universe. Some scrolls are written so that almost every column begins with the word "the king" *(ha-melekh),* and are known as the "the king's scroll".

The Book of Esther inscribed in miniscule lettering, forming the shape of a bear (micrography); Russia, 1870.

Since the word for God does not appear in the Scroll of Esther, artists felt free to illustrate it, and it is the only biblical book in the Jewish tradition whose text is often illuminated and ornamented with gold leaf, miniature paintings, border designs and other fanciful motifs.

80

A papercut *megillah,* Italy, 17th century. At top right, Haman's ten sons on the gallows; top left, Jacob's dream of angels ascending and descending the ladder to heaven.

The practice of ornamenting the first letter of each chapter of the scroll appeared in Southern France and Western Germany in the 12th and 13th centuries, and then spread to Italy in the late 14th and early 15th centuries. This was the great era of Italian manuscript art, and the *Megillah* decorations of this period reflect a high standard of craftsmanship and beauty.

When the Jews moved to Eastern Europe, the decoration of the scroll itself was abandoned in favor of elaborate ornamentation of the case made to contain the scroll. It might be carved of wood, or intricately worked in silver or gold.

Reading the Megillah

Three benedictions of thanksgiving are recited before the *Megillah* is read. The first acknowledges the fact that one has been held worthy to read the sacred book. The second recognizes that God miraculously delivered our ancestors in those days. The third, the *she-heḥeyanu* benediction recited on every festival, expresses gratitude for being alive to celebrate the event.

The blessing which follows the *Megillah* reading praises God

81

the Savior for having fought our battles, judged our disputes, avenged our injuries, and punished our enemies.

Before the reading it is customary to give charity to the poor. This collection, known as *mahazit ha-shekel,* the "half-shekel," is reminiscent of the tax collected for the maintenance of the Temple and its services. The contribution is also called *megillah gelt·* or *igra de-ta'anita* ("*megillah* money" or "fasting profit" referring to the money saved by not eating on the Fast of Esther).

The reading itself follows a special cantillation or melodic pattern. The scroll is spread out and folded over in the form of a "letter", because of the letters sent to the governors concerning the Jews, and the letters sent to the Jews regarding the celebration of Purim.

During the geonic period it became customary for the reader to raise his voice, and for the entire congregation to join him, when reciting the four verses of "redemption" that tell of Mordecai's origin and of his triumph over Haman:

There was a certain Jew in Shushan the castle, whose name was Mordecai the son of Jair the son of Shimei the son of Kish, a Benjamite.

And Mordecai went forth from the presence of the king in royal apparel of blue and white, and with a great crown of gold, and with a robe of fine linen and purple; and the city of Shushan shouted and was glad.

The Jews had light and gladness and joy and honor.

For Mordecai the Jew was next unto King Ahasuerus, and great among the Jews, and accepted of the multitude of his brethren; seeking the good of his people and speaking peace to all his seed.

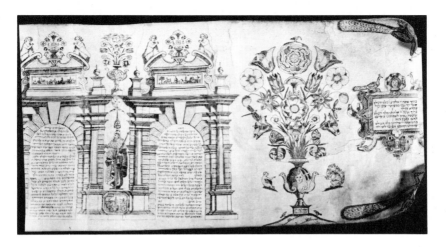

A Scroll of Esther very elaborately illustrated by Shalom Italia whose name is on the neck of the vase. Italia (c.1619 - c.1655), an engraver, etcher and draftsman, was active in Amsterdam for between 8 and 15 years, and this is one example of several *megillot* he produced. A "King's Scroll" from Italy, with each column beginning with the word *ha-melech*.

Another practice is for the reader to recite the tongue-twister names of the ten sons of Haman in one breath to show that they were executed simultaneously. The rabbis have also interpreted this custom as a refusal by Jews to gloat over the downfall of their enemies.

In Hamadan, Persia, the Jews traditionally gather at a site where they believe the graves of Esther and Mordecai to be located, to read the *Megillah* and to recite various prayers. They have a local tradition that their town was the city of Shushan during the days of King Ahasuerus.

The most distinctive feature of the *Megillah* reading is the "blotting out" of Haman's name whenever it is pronounced. This is most often accomplished by rattling a special Purim noise-maker, popularly known by its Yiddish name, *gregger* (Hebrew: *ra'ashan*).

Haman's Name

This custom, of ancient origin, derives from an interpretation of two biblical verses: "Thou shalt wipe out the memory of Amalek", and, "The name of the wicked shall rot." In the Book of Esther Haman is referred to as "the Agagite", which the rabbis interpreted as meaning that he was a descendant of Agag, king of Amalek during the reign of King Saul in Israel. The Amalekites were long-standing enemies of the Jews.

Abudarham, a Spanish-Jewish writer of the 14th century who described the customs connected with Jewish prayer in various countries, relates that in his time children used to make wooden and stone models of Haman and write his name upon them. When the name Haman was mentioned during the reading of the *Megillah,* they would "smite their effigies lustily". In the 16th century, a Jewish author wrote that while the Book of Esther was read "there are some who, as often as they hear Haman named, beat the ground, and make a great murmuring noise in token of cursing him and execrating his memory."

Jews in Eastern Europe used to write the name of Haman on the soles of their shoes, and stamp their feet when hearing his name, thus wiping out the writing. A visitor to a synagogue in London in the early 19th century describes how immigrants from Poland would write Haman's name on a slip of paper and industriously erase it during the reading of the *Megillah*.

The venerable custom of blotting out Haman's name has been updated by 20th century children who gleefully bring such noise-making implements as cap pistols, alarm clocks, and toy trumpets to the *Megillah* reading.

In ancient Persia and Babylonia, an effigy of Haman was burned on Purim. This custom was retained in some communities (Egypt, Kurdistan, Italy) until recent years.

Shabbat Zakhor

The association between Purim and Amalek, noted above, has led to the designation of the Sabbath before Purim as *Shabbat Zakhor*, the Sabbath of Remembrance (*zakhor* = remember). The name derives from the Torah reading of this Sabbath:

> Remember what Amalek did to you on your journey, after you left Egypt; how, undeterred by fear of God, he surprised you on the march, when you were famished and weary, and cut down all the stragglers in your rear. Therefore, when the Lord your God grants you safety in the land that the Lord your God is giving you as a hereditary portion, you shall blot out the memory of Amalek from under heaven. Do not forget!

This is the only Torah reading of the year which is explicitly ordained in the Torah itself. The reading from the Prophets echoes this theme. It is from the First Book of Samuel, chapter 15, which begins: "Thus says the Lord of hosts: I remember that which Amalek did to Israel . . . when he came up out of Egypt."

Liturgy

The enmity between Amalek and Israel became a symbol in

86

Purim in a *shtetl* ; painting by Marc Chagall.

Purim noisemakers. Above: wood, inscribed with
Hebrew words *arur haman*, Germany, 18th century;
below: silver, showing Haman leading Mordecai,
New York, 20th century.

Judaism for the eternal battle of God against the forces of evil,
and the figure of Haman in particular came to stand for the
embodiment of evil in every generation, an evil from which the

Jewish people will eventually be saved. (During the Hitler period, Jews frequently referred to that arch-enemy of the Jews as "Haman".)

Thus, the Mishnah established that the reading from the Torah on Purim was to include three sections from Exodus, chapter 17, which describe the attack of the Amalekites upon the Israelites.

The reading of Psalm 22 is also part of the holiday service. This psalm is prefaced by the dedicatory phrase "For the leader upon *ayelet ha-shaḥar* (the morning star)." It is traditionally held that "morning star" refers to Queen Esther (who was as beautiful as the morning star), and that this was the prayer she offered after she had completed her three-day fast, and before she sought an audience with the king.

The moving language of the psalm opens with unforgettable phrases:

> My God, my God, why has Thou forsaken me . . . I call by day but Thou answerest not; and at night and there is no surcease for me. Yet Thou art holy, O Thou who art enthroned upon the praises of Israel. In Thee did our fathers trust; they trusted and Thou didst deliver them. Unto Thee they cried and escaped; in Thee they did trust and were not ashamed. . . .

The poignant despair of the opening is balanced at the close of the psalm by the exultation of faith rewarded:

> For the kingdom is the Lord's . . . it shall be told of the Lord unto the next generation; they shall come and shall declare His righteousness unto a people that shall be born, that He hath done it.

An addition to the *Amidah* and the grace after meals on Purim is *Al ha-Nissim*

"New Moon Prayers",
painting by A. Bender,
late 19th century.

Hasidim dancing
around the Lag
ba-Omer bonfire
at Meron, 1972.

Tree planting traditionally carried out by school children in Israel as part of the Tu bi-Shevat ceremonies. School children seen here are planting trees in Arad, 1969.

the *Al ha-Nissim* ("For the Miracles") prayer, which is also recited on Ḥanukkah, a festival which commemorates another miracle.

In contrast to the sharing of *Al ha-Nissim* by both Ḥanukkah and Purim, the *Hallel* (Psalms of Praise) which is said on Ḥanukkah is not recited on Purim. The traditional explanation is that *Hallel* is appropriate for the spiritual redemption marked by Ḥanukkah, the Feast of the Rededication of the Temple. The purely physical redemption of the Jews, marked by Purim, the Feast of Lots, is celebrated more appropriately with a festive meal, the *se'udah*.

Hallel

Gifts

The Scroll of Esther relates that after the Jews of Persia were saved from destruction, they celebrated with gladness and feasting, and by "sending portions to one another and gifts to the poor." Based on this verse, the rabbis legislated that on Purim one must send at least two "portions" of delicacies – baked goods, candies, wine or liquor – to friends, and give a present of money to at least two poor men. The "sending of portions" is known by the Hebrew term *mishlo'aḥ manot*, which has been changed by popular usage into *shelaḥ-mones*. The law is that these gifts should not be handed over personally but by a messenger thus fulfilling the term "sending."

89

It is the children's task, on Purim morning, to carry the trays with *shelah-mones* to the homes of relatives and friends, to return home with reciprocated delicacies, and probably with their mouths stuffed with goodies to eat on the way. Purim morning in Israel is particularly colorful, as the children, dressed in costumes, hurry through the streets with their *mishlo'ah manot* packages.

In some communities, special plates, often made of pewter, were kept for the purpose of sending Purim gifts. They were frequently engraved with quotations from the Scroll of Esther

A silver plate in form of a fish (Pisces) used for *mishloah manot* , Austria, 19th century.

A *mishloaḥ manot* engraved with verses and scenes from the
megillah ; tin, Germany, 18th century.

and with scenes from the Purim story. In Near Eastern Jewish
communities, *mishlo'aḥ manot* include home-made sugar-starch
fingers in various colors. Non-Jews in those countries call Purim
'id al-sukar, the sugar festival.

Although every Jewish holiday was an occasion for giving
charity, special collections were made at Purim to provide
dowries for poor brides, and to ransom Jewish captives. As early
as the days of the Mishnah, a collection was made to provide the

91

needy with funds so that they could enjoy a Purim *se'udah*. In the words of the Talmud: "Purim collections are exclusively for Purim."

Feasts and Foods
Because the Scroll of Esther states that the holiday of Purim is to be celebrated in feasting and gladness, the sages established that every Jew is to partake in a special Purim meal *(se'udah)* which is to begin while there is yet daylight. As noted above, this is as

"Purim at Home," an oil painting by Moritz Oppenheim. The strolling Purim *shpilers* are entertaining the family, for which they will be suitably rewarded.

Wooden pastry forms for Purim cookies. The form on the right depicts Mordechai and Haman, and that on the lower left shows fish which are the zodiac sign for the month of Adar. Holland, 18th century.

much a duty to be fulfilled on Purim as the recitation of the *hallel* is a Ḥanukkah obligation.

The Purim festival has a long culinary history. The humorous *Massekhet Purim*, written by Kalonymus ben Kalonymus (14th century), records a Purim menu listing 27 different meat dishes.

The most famous of the traditional foods associated with Purim are the three-cornered pastries made of sweet dough, and filled with a mixture of poppyseeds and honey, called *mohn* (from the German) or *pereg* (Hebrew). The eating of poppyseeds and honey as a Purim sweetmeat was noted as early as the 12th century in a religious poem written by Abraham Ibn Ezra.

Hamentaschen

These cakes, made by all Jewish communities, are known by a variety of names, and are supposed to represent Haman's hat, Haman's pockets, or Haman's ears. The "pockets" refer to the villain's pockets which were stuffed with the bribe money he offered to King Ahasuerus. The "ears" may refer to the punishment of criminals whose ears were cut off before they were hanged. In Yiddish they are called *hamantaschen;* in Hebrew they are *oznei haman.* They may also be filled with *povidl,* prune jam, to commemorate the rescue of Jews in Bohemia in the early 18th century, when a plum merchant was saved from persecution.

93

A poster
announcing a
Purim ball in
New York City
in 1836. The
text is humorous
with what must
obviously be
topical allusions
(left).
A Purim ball in
New York City
(opposite).

94

Other traditional sweets include the *mohn plaetzen* or poppy-seed cookies eaten by Jews from Western Europe and the *ciambella di Purim* enjoyed by Italian Jews. Fried pastries sprinkled with sugar are called *hamansoren* in Holland, *haman-muetzen* in Germany, *schunzuchen* in Switzerland and French-Lorraine, *heizenblauzen* in Austria, *diples* in Greece, *shamleya* in Turkey, and *orecchie de aman* in Italy.

The Purim ḥallah loaf (often given the Russian name *keylitsh*) is giant-sized and braided, representing the long ropes used to hang Haman.

Sephardi communities bake sweet cakes filled with almonds or other nuts, make marzipan candies, special *puralis* cake containing a whole egg, and various sorts of pancakes. In Persia it was customary to serve *ha'alva kashka,* a spiced dessert, after the

95

Megillah reading. In Salonika and Istanbul women baked *kulimas, barikas*, or *sambusachkhavsh* — pastries of dough filled with meat.

Among European Jews it is traditional to eat *kreplach*, small pouches made of dough and filled with chopped meat. Folklore establishes that *kreplach* are to be eaten whenever there is "beating and banging." Thus, in some Jewish communities they are part of the meal on the eve of the Day of Atonement

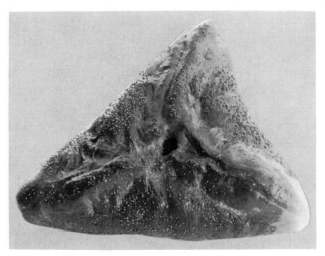

Hamantasch, the traditional Purim pastry.

(because of the biblical punishment of one's sins by 39 stripes and the beating of the breast during the liturgical confession), on Hoshannah Rabbah, the last day of the Festival of Sukkot (when the willow branches are beaten), and on Purim (because of the banging when Haman's name is mentioned).

Some groups of Jews eat turkey on Purim, because in various languages that bird is known as the "cock of India", and Ahasuerus "ruled from India even unto Ethiopia". Other com-

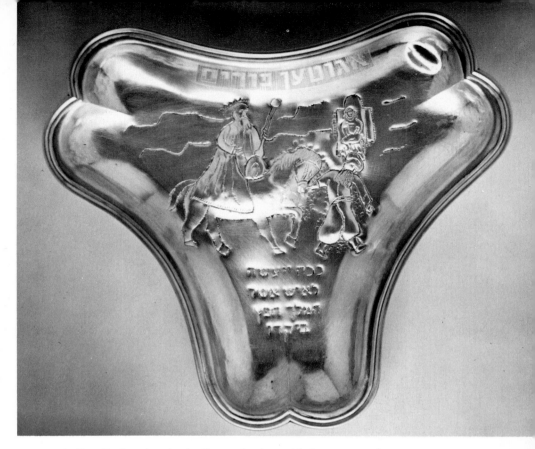

A silver Purim plate in the form of a three sided *Hamantasch*.
Haman is leading Mordechai on the king's horse while slops are
being thrown on his head. This is according to a midrash.

munities eat boiled beans and peas, as a reminder of the cereals
Daniel ate in the Persian king's palace in order to avoid breaking
the dietary laws.

In contrast to the feasting of Purim itself, it is customary to *The Fast*
fast on the preceding day, the thirteenth of Adar, in memory of *of Esther*
Queen Esther's fast. An eighth century document is the earliest
to record this custom. If the thirteenth of Adar falls on a

Sabbath, the fast is moved to the preceding Thursday (rather than being postponed to the next day, which would be Purim itself). Special penitential prayers *(selihot)* are recited, in addition to those of a regular fast-day, and the fast-day portion of the Torah is read.

While various authorities hold the Fast of Esther to be less obligatory than other fast-days, some Jews, particularly those of Persian origin, continue to observe it strictly, and consider it as binding as the fast of the Day of Atonement.

Purim clowns; woodcut, early 18th century.

In a most uncharacteristically Jewish fashion, Purim is the *The Joy of* one day during the year when the individual is urged not only to *Drinking* feast, but also to drink — and to excess. One talmudic scholar proclaimed that at the Purim *se'udah* one should drink until he cannot distinguish between the phrases "cursed be Haman" and "blessed be Mordecai"! Not content to leave this pleasant rule alone, the rabbis sought to emphasize it by explaining that in *gematria* (the substitution of a numerical equivalent for every Hebrew letter) the numerical value of each of these phrases totals 502. Thus the phrases are equal to one another, and when drunk, a man cannot tell one phrase from the other.

Purim Shpils

The merriment of the synagogue service on Purim, enhanced by the joy resulting from food and drink, finds expression in the *Purim shpil*, or Purim play. As far as can be told, the earliest type of such a play consisted of boys and girls dressing up in costumes and making the rounds of Jewish homes, singing jingles, reciting poems, and asking for money or refreshments. Such entertainment was widespread among Ashkenazi communities as early as the mid-16th century. The poems were mainly paraphrases of the Book of Esther and parodies of other holy texts and prayers, such as a *"Kiddush"* or "sermon." Other *Purim shpils* might make humerous comments on contemporary Jewish life, or imitate the idosyncracies of the rabbi and his disciples. These satires, and the physical expression of "beating" Haman, served

"Purimspiel," an oil painting by Yankel Adler, 1931.

Masked children on a
Jerusalem street, 1963 (left).
A Purim party in a kinder-
garten in Israel, 1960 (below).

as safety valves for letting off steam within the framework of the
rigidly controlled Jewish life in the East European Diaspora.

Before World War II, Jewish players performed lengthy folk
dramas in many East European towns and villages on Purim, or
during the entire month of Adar. Even in Orthodox communities
the taboo on acting and on the use of masks was lifted during
this period to allow for stage performances. However, the
religious authorities frequently prohibited men from performing
feminine roles. The *Purim shpils* were very often acted by young-
sters of the lower social classes, tailor's apprentices, and laborers.

In Western Europe and the United States the masks and
costumes of the *Purim shpil* assumed the form of masquerade
balls held on Purim, with the income derived from the festivities
earmarked for a communal charity. Children's masquerade
parties are still sponsored by Jewish community groups.

The costume party is a favored Purim festivity in Israel,
among both young and old. Costumed children in particular turn

100

out to throng the streets of the towns and cities on Purim, which is an official school holiday.

Another traditional custom, that of electing a Purim King or Purim Queen, probably originated in Provence (France) in the 14th century. When the Jews were expelled from Provence in 1496, the custom was brought to Italy. Later, in the *yeshivot* of Eastern Europe, a Purim Rabbi was elected. In the United States and in Israel, "Queen Esther" is frequently chosen in a Purim beauty contest.

The Purim King or Queen

All of these customs — drinking, masquerading, presenting amateur theatricals or satiric skits, choosing a mock king, queen or rabbi — are similar to customs associated among other religious groups with the "Carnival" which is also held in early spring.

A Purim *shpil* ; drawing by an unknown artist in Bohemia - Moravia.

פורים וול ז ני גבט איד ... לוי טו אן ליבר יתי דרי ... ט סדרה !
ויין . אוג ד לר חן סרחטיי דיא בנדה אוני גיק ורק תין
כריב לוט יך ניס תובר אנוגר גווינקיט . ' אוני וגו טריד דריא בכית :

A woodcut of a Purim *shpil* in the Middle Ages.

In 1912, a great Purim *adloyada* carnival was held in Tel *Adloyada*
Aviv. It consisted of a procession of decorated floats and bands
which marched through the main streets while the populace of
the first all-Jewish city in the modern world turned out to watch.
Since then an *adloyada* has been held intermittently in various
towns in Israel.

The name *adloyada* is derived from the rabbinic saying,
discussed above, that one should drink "until one no longer
knows" (in the Aramaic of the Talmud, *ad de-lo yada*) the
difference between "blessed be Mordecai" and "cursed be
Haman."

102

Two floats from *Adloyada* processions in Tel Aviv, 1955 and 1968.
Crowd control was a serious problem.

In the Arts

The figure of Esther has enjoyed great popularity among writers, artists and musicians, who have produced works presenting her feminine modesty, courage, and self-sacrifice. From the Renaissance onwards she has figured in Jewish plays intended for performance on Purim, and Christian dramas which established Esther as a model of Christian womanly virtues. Because of Esther's association with King Ahasuerus, the plays often contained marked political undertones reflecting dissatisfaction with whatever king was then ruling.

An early reproduction of scenes from the Book of Esther appears in the cycle of paintings found in the third-century synagogue at Dura-Europos. In medieval Christian art Esther was a familiar figure. Her intercession with Ahaseuerus on behalf of the Jews was associated with the Virgin Mary's mediation with God on behalf of mankind. Scenes depicting episodes in the

"Haman Falls into Disgrace," pen drawing by Rembrandt.

Scroll of Esther appear in murals and tapestries in cathedrals throughout Europe, executed by artists such as Botticelli, Filippino Lippi, Tintoretto, Paolo Veronese, Rubens and Rembrandt.

Perhaps the best-known musical work using the theme of the Purim story is Handel's oratorio, *Haman and Mordecai,* which was presented at the King's Theatre in London in 1732, and was his first English composition in oratorio form. The most notable modern work on the subject is Darius Milhaud's opera *Esther de Carpentras,* which dramatized the staging of an old Provençal Purim play and the threat posed by a bishop who sought to convert the Jews.

Special Purims

Because Purim commemorates an occasion when the Jews were threatened with destruction and were saved by a miracle, the name "Purim" has been lent to other occasions when a particular Jewish community or family escaped destruction in one form or another. Each year these days of deliverance are celebrated as festivals by the descendants of those originally involved. Some mark an escape from a natural disaster such as a plague, an earthquake or a major conflagration; others commemorate release from tyrannical rulers, from prison sentences or from threat of war. Each of these Purims emphasizes the spiritual lesson of the first Purim, namely that the unseen hand of God guides the destiny of the Jewish people.

These special Purims, which may total over one hundred in number, are celebrated in a fashion similar to the original Purim. Those who observe it do not engage in work. Special psalms and prayers are recited in the synagogue. Frequently a special *Megillah,* written in the style of the Book of Esther, is read. The participants partake in a feast, and give charity to the poor.

It is clear that throughout the Diaspora and across the centuries Purim has retained its significance for the Jews.

Through a process of historical reinterpretation it has provided a message of faith in God's eternal watchfulness over His people, and hope for their eventual redemption. The specific events of Purim provided an example of God's solemn vow to destroy Amalek, the symbol of evil. Many seemingly divine interventions in the fate of beleaguered Jewish communities have been called "Purim," bringing new meaning to the words of the Scroll of Esther: "These days of Purim shall not disappear from among the Jews, nor the memorial of them perish from their seed."

A *megillah* prepared for the special Purim instituted in 1758 in Ferrara, to celebrate an escape from a great fire. The word Ferrara in Hebrew can be seen in the next to last line, middle column.

מגלת פרס

עַל הנס שנעשה כעיר **בצרה** יע"א
יוס ב' ניסן שנת **התק"לה**
והזספנו כה את המעשה אשר נעשה
כזמן ההוא   ונס מעשה שני יוס הנס
העושיס פה **בגדאד** יע"א כקלדה
י"ר שנשמח בביאת הגואל נרק כב"א :

פה   **בגדאד**   יע"א

שנת שמחה **וש'ש'ון** ליהו'ריס לפ"ק

בדפוס ח' עזרא דנגור ס"ט

Title page of a *megillah* for a special Purim
originating in Basra, 1775.

Purim of . . .	Observed on	Established in	Reason for Observance
Algiers (called Purim Edom)	4th Heshvan	1540	Saved from destruction in Spanish-Algerian wars of 1516–1517 and 1542
Algiers (called Purim Tammuz)	11th Tammuz	1774	Saved from danger.
Alessandria Della Paglia (Italy)	25th Av	1779	Saved from massacre.
Ditto	2nd Heshvan	1797	Saved from riots during revolutionary war.
Ancona	21st Tevet	1690	Saved from earthquake.
Ancona	15th Tishri	1741	Synagogue escaped destruction by fire.
Ancona	24th Adar	1775	Jewish quarter saved from conflagration.
Ancona	12th Shevat	1797	Saved from riots in revolutionary war.
Angora/Ankara/(called: Purim Angora or Purim Sari-Kiz)	21st Elul	?	Saved from blood libel accusation.
Angora, called Purim Abazza	11th Iyyar	?	?
Angora, called Purim de la Turquito	14th Tammuz	1775	Saved from blood libel accusation.
Avignon	24th Tammuz	?	?
Avignon	28th Shevat	1757	Escaped dangers of a riot.
Baghdad	11th Av	1733	Relieved from Persian oppression.
Belgrade	19th Sivan	1822	Saved from destruction during Turko-Serbian war.
Breche (Champagne, France)	14th Adar	1191	Chief Jew-baiter executed
Cairo	18th Shevat	?	?
Cairo, called Purim Miẓrayim	28th Adar	1524	Saved from extermination.
Candia (Crete)	18th Tammuz	1583	Saved from collective punishment for treason, during Turco-Venetian conflict
Carpentras	16th Kislev	1512	Saved from riot.
Ditto	9th Nisan	1692	Saved from annihilation.
Ditto, called Yom va-Yosha	21st Nisan	1651	Saved from threat of massacre.
Casablanca, called Purim Hitler	2nd Kislev	1943	Escape from riot and Nazi occupation.
Castille (Spain) called Purim Martinez	1st Adar	1339	Saved from annihilation following accusations by Jew-baiter Gonzales Martinez, king's adviser.
Cavaillon (Provence)	25th Iyyar	1631	Plague ended.
Ditto	29th Sivan	1677	Saved from blood libel accusation.
Cento (Italy)	12th Av	1820	Escaped from fire.
Chieri (Italy)	1st Av	1797	Saved from danger of war.
Chios (Greece), called Purim de la Senora ("Purim of the Good Lady")	8th Iyyar	1595 (or 1820)?	Saved from death during Franco-Turkish war.
Cuneo (Italy)	5th Kislev	1799	Synagogue saved from destruction by shell.
Ettingen (Germany)	18th Iyyar	1690	Saved from destruction by enemies.
Ditto	29th Sivan	1713	?
Ferrara	24th Kislev	?	Saved from destruction by fire.
Ditto	18th Iyyar	1799	Escaped war riots.
Fez	22nd Kislev	1840	Saved from destruction.
Florence	27th Sivan	1791	Escaped sacking and riots.
Fossano (Italy)	18th Nisan	1796	Saved from bomb explosion during war.
Frankfort on the Main, also called: Purim Winz or Purim Fettmilch	20th Adar	1616	Expelled Jews readmitted to town and chief Jew-baiter, Fettmilch, executed.
Fulda	15th Elul	?	?
Gumeldjina (Thrace) called: Purim de los ladrones ("Purim of the thiefs")	22nd Elul	1786	Saved from collective punishment for allegedly instigating robbers to sack town.
Hebron	1st Av	?	Saved from collective punishment and execution by Ibrahim Pasha.
Ditto, called Purim Takka ("Window Purim")	14th Tevet	1741	Saved from annihilation by miraculous find of ransom money on the windowsill of synagogue
Ivrea (Italy)	1st Shevat	1797	Escaped plundering during revolutionary war.
Komotini (Gumurjina, Gumuldjina) (Greece)	22nd Elul	1768	Saved from destruction during Turkish suppression of Greek revolt.

108

Purim of ...	Observed on	Established in	Reason for Observance
Kovno	7th Adar (II)	1783	Privileges of civic freedom granted by King Poniatowski.
Leghorn	12th Shevat	1742	Saved from destruction in earthquake.
Ditto	25th Tevet	1810	Plague ends.
Ditto	16th Adar	1813	?
Lepanto (Greece)	11th Tevet	1699	Saved from destruction during Turkish war.
Medzibozs (Poland)	11th Tevet	1648 or 1649	Saved from annihilation by Chmielnicki's bands.
Mestislaw (Russia)	4th Shevat	1744	Saved from slaughter by Cossacks.
Ditto	3rd Kislev	1844	Saved from collective punishment for alleged rebellion against authorities.
Morocco	13th Nisan	1771	Saved from annihilation.
Narbonne	20th Adar	1236	Saved from riots.
Oran	6th Av	1830	Saved from massacre before arrival of French troops.
Ostraha	23rd Nisan	1734 or 1768	Saved from pogrom.
Ditto	7th Tammuz	1792	Saved from destruction during Russo-Polish war.
Padua	Shabbat "Toledot"	1795	Saved from fire.
Ditto, called Purim di Buda	10th Elul	1684	Saved from massacre during Austro-Turkish war (in Budapest).
Ditto, called Purim dei Sassi (?)	Shabbat "Bo"	1748	?
Ditto, called Purim di fuoco ("Fire Purim")	11th Sivan	1795	Saved from conflagration.
Pesaro/see also: Urbino and Senigallia	?	1799	Escaped damages of war.
Pitigliano (Italy)	15th Tammuz	1757	Collapse of school roof, no casualties.
Ditto	15th Sivan	1799	Saved from damages during revolutionary war.
Posen	1st Heshvan	1704	Saved from death during Polish-Swedish war.
Prague	14th Heshvan	1620	Saved from sacking and riots by protection of Emperor Ferdinand II.
Ditto, called Vorhang Purim ("Curtain Purim")	22nd Tevet	1622	Beadle of synagogue saved from hanging for keeping stolen curtains.
Purim Byzanc (observed by Jews of Thrace)	14th Adar	1574	Saved from extermination.
Ragusa	?	1631	Saved from accusation of blood libel.
Rhodes	14th Adar	1840	Saved from annihilation.
Ritova (Lithuania) called Purim Jeroboam b. Nebat	14th Adar	1863	Jew-baiter Count Aginsky died.
Rome	1st Shevat	1793	Ghetto saved from assault and fire.
Sa'na	18th Adar	?	Saved from extermination.
Sarajevo	4th Heshvan	1807	10 leaders of Jewish community freed from prison and saved from execution.
Ditto	4th Heshvan	1820	Saved from annihilation by despotic ruler.
Senigallia (Italy)/see also: Urbino and Pesaro	15th Sivan	1799	Saved from annihilation during war by escaping to Ancona.
Sermide (Italy)	25th Tammuz	1809	Saved from earthquake.
Shiraz, called Purim Mo'ed Katan	2nd Heshvan	1200 or 1400	Permitted to practice Judaism after having been forced to convert to Islam.
Spoleto	21st Sivan	1797	Saved from annihilation during revolutionary war.
Ditto	7th Adar	?	?
Sienna	15th Sivan	1799	Saved from destruction during revolution.
Syracuse (Sicily), called Purim Saragossa	17th Shevat	1425	Saved from destruction for alleged treason by honoring King Alfonso with empty cases of Torah Scrolls.
Tetuan and Tangiers, called Purim de las bombas, or Purim de los Christianos,	2nd Elul	1578	Saved from destruction during Moroccan-Portuguese war.

Purim of . . .	Observed on	Established in	Reason for Observance
Tiberias	4th Kislev	1742	Siege temporarily lifted
Ditto	7th Elul	1743	Siege abandoned
Trieste	14th Adar	1833	Leading Jew-baiter died.
Tripoli and Tunisia	25th Shevat	?	?
Ditto, called Purim Sheriff or Purim Kadebani ("False Purim")	24th Tevet	1705	Saved from destruction by hostile ruler, Khalil Pasha.
Ditto, called Purim Borghel	29th Tevet	1793	Saved from destruction during occupation by Borghel Pasha of Turkey.
Tunisia, called: Purim Sheleg ("Purim of Snow")	24th Tevet	1891	Jewish quarter saved from natural disaster.
Tunisia	15th Shevat	?	?
Turino	1st Av	1797	Saved from war and sacking.
Urbino	11th Sivan	1799	Saved from war and riots.
Verona	20th Tammuz	1607	Permission granted to lock ghetto gates from inside instead of from outside.
Vidin, Bulgaria, called Purim de los borrachones ("Purim of the Drunken")	4th and 5th Heshvan or 9th—10th	1806	Saved from annihilation following accusation that the ruler had been poisoned by his Jewish physician.
Ditto	2nd Adar	1878	Saved from destruction during Russo-Turkish (Balkan) war.
Vilna	15th Av	1794	Saved from destruction during Russo-Polish war.
Zborow (Galicia)	12th Tevet	?	Saved from annihilation because of blood libel accusation.

Family purims

Altschul family of Prague	22nd Tevet	1623	Head of family, Ḥanokh Moses, saved from death.
Brandeis family of Jungbunzlau (Bohemia), called Povidl Purim "Plum Jam Purim"	10th Adar	1731	David Brandeis and family saved from accusation of having killed gentiles by poisoning plum jam.
Danzig family of Vilna, called Pulverpurim ("Powder Purim")	15th Kislev	1804	Family of Abraham Danzig, author of *Ḥayyei Adam*, saved from explosion of magnesium.
Elyashar family of Jerusalem	2nd Nisan	?	Saved from death.
Heller family of Prague	1st Adar	1629	Head of family, Yom Tov Lipmann, rabbi of Prague saved from death sentence.
Jonathan ben Jacob of Fulda (Germany)	17th Tammuz	?	?
Maimon family of Lithuania	?	1750	Grandfather of Solomon Maimon saved from death sentence for blood libel.
Meyuhas family of Jerusalem	16th Adar	1724	Head of family, Raphael Meyuhas, escaped death by highwaymen.
Samuel Ha-Nagid of Spain	1st Elul	1039	Saved from death plot of conspirators.
Segal family of Cracow	1st Iyyar	1657	Family saved from drowning in river while escaping from pogrom.
Treves family (?)	Shabbat "Va-Yeze"	1758	Escaped from fire.

The Karaites observe a special Purim on 1st Shevat, in memory of the release from prison of one of their leaders, Yerushalmi. The exact date of the event is unknown.
The followers of *Shabbetai Ẓevi observed a special Purim on 15th Kislev, because on this day in 1648, Shabbetai Ẓevi proclaimed himself Messiah.

A German - Jewish family celebrating Ḥanukkah.
Painting by Moritz Oppenheim, 1880.

Adar, twelfth month of the Jewish year (February–March).

Al ha-Nissim, prayer of thanksgiving for miracles, recited during the *Amidah* and the grace after meals on Ḥanukkah and Purim.

Amidah, main prayer recited at all services; also known as *Shemoneh Esreh* (18 benedictions).

Ashkenazi (pl. Ashkenazim), German or West-, Central-, or East-European Jew(s), as contrasted with Sephardi(m).

Av, fifth month of the Jewish year (July–August).

Elul, sixth month of the Jewish year (August–September).

Ereẓ Israel, the Land of Israel.

Haftarah, portion from the Prophets, read in the synagogue on the Sabbath, festivals and fast days.

Hallel, songs of praise, Psalms 113–118 recited in the liturgy on festivals.

Iyyar, second month of the Jewish year (April–May).

Kabbalists, mystics; Safed was an important center of this group in the 16th century.

Kiddush, prayer recited over a goblet of wine to sanctify the Sabbaths and festivals.

Kiddush levanah, sanctification of the moon.

Kislev, ninth month of the Jewish year (November–December).

Ma'ariv, evening prayer service.

Megillah, scroll. (*Megillat Ester* – Scroll of Esther).

Menorah, candelabrum; seven-branched lamp used in the Temple; eight-branched lamp used on Ḥanukkah.

Minḥah, the afternoon prayer service.

Mishnah, codification of Jewish Oral Law, completed in the third century c.e.

Mitzvah, biblical or rabbinic injunction.

Musaf, additional prayer service on Sabbaths and festivals.

Nisan, first month of the Jewish year (March–April).

Omer, period of 49 days between Passover and Shavuot; marked by semi-mourning practices.

Passover, festival beginning on the fifteenth of Nisan, lasting seven days in Israel, eight days in the Diaspora, commemorating the Exodus from Egypt.

Rosh Ha-Shanah, New Year, two day holiday at the beginning of the month of Tishrei (September–October).

Sanhedrin, Jewish high court in Temple times.

Seder, the ceremony on the first night (in the Diaspora first two nights) of Passover.

Seliḥot, penitential prayers.

Sephardi (pl. Sephardim), Jews of Spain and Portugal and their descendants wherever resident; loosely used for Jews of Oriental countries. Contrasted with Ashkenazi(m).

Se'udah, festive meal; *se'udat mitzvah,* a festive meal required by *halakhah* (law), as part of the observance of a festival.

Shalom aleikhem, phrase of greeting; literally, peace be with you.

Shavuot, Pentecost, Feast of Weeks; celebrated one day in Israel and two days in the Diaspora in the month of Sivan.

She-heḥeyanu, benediction expressing gratitude for being alive to celebrate an event (such as a festival).

Shekhinah, Divine Presence.

Shevat, eleventh month of the Jewish year (January–February).

Shofar, ram's horn, ceremonially blown on festive occasions.

Shulḥan Arukh, Code of Jewish law; compiled in 16th century by Joseph Caro.

Sukkot, Tabernacles, festival beginning on the fifteenth of the month of Tishrei (September–October).

Tahanun, prayer of supplication.

Talmud, compendium of commentary on the Mishnah; completed in the 6th century c.e.

Tishrei, seventh month of the Jewish year (September–October).

Yeshivah, (pl. *yeshivot),* academy devoted mainly to the study of Talmud and rabbinics.

Yom Kippur, Day of Atonement. The most solemn day of the Jewish calendar.

Zohar, mystical commentary on the Pentateuch; main textbook of Kabbalah (Jewish mystic tradition).

ABBREVIATIONS OF SOURCES

Bible

Gen.	– Genesis	Sam.	– Samuel	Esth.	– Esther
Ex.	– Exodus	Is.	– Isaiah	Dan.	– Daniel
Lev.	– Leviticus	Zech.	– Zechariah	Neh.	– Nehemiah
Num.	– Numbers	Prov.	– Proverbs	Macc.	– Maccabees
Deut.	– Deuteronomy				

Talmud[1]

TJ	– *Jerusalem Talmud*[2]				
Ar.	– *Arakhin*	Hul.	– *Hullin*	Pes.	– *Pesahim*
Av. Z.	– *Avodah Zarah*	Kel.	– *Kelaim*	RH	– *Rosh ha-Shanah*
Ber.	– *Berakhot*	Kid.	– *Kiddushin*	San.	– *Sanhedrin*
BK	– *Baba Kama*	Ma'as	– *Ma'aserot*	Shab.	– *Shabbath*
BM	– *Baba Mezia*	Meg.	– *Megillah*	Sof.	– *Soferim*
Git.	– *Gittin*	Men.	– *Menahot*	Suk.	– *Sukkah*
Hag.	– *Hagigah*	MK	– *Mo'ed Katan*	Ta'an.	– *Ta'anit*
		Ned.	– *Nedarim*	Yev.	– *Yevamot*

Later Authorities

Yad	– Maimonides, *Yad Hazakah*
Sh. Ar., OH	– *Shulhan Arukh, Orah Hayyim*

---

[1] References to the Mishnah are in the form Git. 10:6 (i.e., *Tractate Gittin*, chapter 10, Mishnah 6); references to the Gemara are in the form Git. 64a (i.e., *Tractate Gittin*, page 64, first side).

[2] Otherwise all Talmud references are to the Babylonian Talmud.

SOURCES

116

49   presents to teachers — Solis-Cohen, *Ḥanukkah,* p. 103

49   "meals are to be . . . " — Sh. Ar., OH 670:2

50   Nicanor — I Macc. 7:49; II Macc. 15:36

50   "Nicanor Day" — *Megillah Ta'anit* 12

52   Ḥanukkah . . . card playing — Solis-Cohen, *Ḥanukkah,* p. 104—5

53   "a glass lantern" — Kel. 2:4

53   metal lamps — Shab. 44a; Ḥul. 9a; Pes. 14a

54   "Blessed are you . . . " Deut. 28:6

57   Hannah . . . Samuel — I Sam. 2:5

60   defensive . . . Sabbath — *Tarbiẓ,* 30 (1961), p. 243—4

62   Louis D. Brandeis — cited in Solis-Cohen, *Ḥannukah,* p. xix

63   listed . . . Mishnah — RH 1:1

63   Talmud . . . New Year — RH 7a

63   The first of Tishrei — RH 3a-b; Git. 8:5

63   "all the world . . . " — RH 1:2

63   terms of rainfall — RH 14a

63   the winter season — RH 1:2; Ma'as. 1

64   "Today water . . . " — Harkavi, *Teshuvot ha-Geonim,* p. 199

64   no penitential prayers — Suk. 45b; TJ Av. 5:1; Sh. Ar., OH 131:6, 572:3

69   When in your war . . . — Deut. 20:19—20

69   The Holy One . . . — *Midrash Tanḥuma, Kedoshim*

69   "If you hold a sapling . . . " — *Avot de Rabbi Natan,* 52

70   "When one chops . . . " — *Pirkei de Rabbi Eliezer,* 34

70   when the Messiah appears — Midrash to Prov. 9:2

71   "When Adar begins . . . " — Ta'an. 29a

74   "Day of Mordecai" — II Macc. 15:36

75   priests . . . leave . . . . duties — Meg. 3a—b

76   Megillah is not read — Meg. 6b

76   Persian kings . . . wives — Herodotus, *History,* 3:84

78   Recent literary research — Bickerman, *Four Strange Books of the Bible*

79   "Lots" . . . Day of Atonement — see Lev. 16:8

79   reading . . . eve — Meg. 4a

79   Women are exempt — Meg 4a; Ar. 3a

82   *maḥazit ha-shekel* — Sh. Ar., OH 694:1

82   form of a "letter" — Yad, Megillah 2:12

82   There was a certain Jew . . . — Esth. 2:5

82   And Mordecai . . . — Esth. 8:15

READING LIST

Encyclopaedia Judaica, Jerusalem, 1972, under: Av, Fifteenth of, Calendar, Ḥanukkah, Independence Day, Lag ba-Omer, *Megillah, Menorah,* New Moon, *Omer,* Purim, Scroll of Esther, Shevat, Fifteenth of, Yom Ha-Zikkaron.

Doniach, N.S., *Purim,* Philadelphia, 1933.
Edidin, Ben M., *Jewish Holidays and Festivals,* New York, 1940.
Gaster, T.H., *Festivals of the Jewish Year,* New York, 1955.
—— , *Purim and Hanukkah,* New York, 1950.
Goodman, P., *The Purim Anthology,* Philadelphia, 1960.
—— , *Rejoice in Thy Festival,* New York, 1956.
Lehrman, S.M., *The Jewish Festivals,* London, 1938.
Newman, A., *Acknowledge the Miracle, Independence Day Anthology with Selected Prayers,* Jerusalem, 1957.
Pearl, C., *Guide to the Minor Festivals and Feasts,* London, 1963.
Schauss, H., *The Jewish Festivals,* Cincinnati, 1938 (paperback, 1968).
Solis-Cohen, E., *Ḥanukkah,* Philadelphia, 1955.
Vainstein, Y., *The Cycle of the Jewish Year,* Jerusalem, 1953.

Tel Aviv, Israel Government Press Office, facing p. 1, 15, 18, 24, 26, 28, 61, 68 (right), 100 (right), 103 (top).
Jerusalem, Israel Government Coins and Medals Corporation, p. 1, 19.
Ardmore, Pa., Sigmund Harrison Collection, p. 5.
J. Bodenschatz, *Kirchliche Verfassung der heutigen Juden,* Frankfort and Leipzig, 1748, p. 8.
London, British Museum, p. 10.
Amsterdam, Jewish Museum, p. 13.
Photo David Harris, Jerusalem, p. 16, 89; color: pl. 5.
Jerusalem, Keren Hayesod Photo Archives, p. 23.
Jerusalem, Jewish National and University Library, p. 25, 40, 66, 78, 98, 102.
N. Avigad, Hebrew University, Jerusalem, p. 34 (right).
Jerusalem, Yad Vashem Archives, p. 34 (left).
Paris, Musée de Cluny, p. 35.
Photo Yizhak Amit, Kibbutz Zorah, p. 38.
Jerusalem, Israel Museum, p. 42, 55 (bottom left), 77, 90, 91, 93 (left), 101, 111; color: pl. 1, 2 (right).
Tel Aviv, Einhorn Collection, p. 43, 55 (top right, center left).
Jerusalem, Sir Isaac and Lady Wolfson Museum, p. 44, 51 (right), 87, 93 (right); color: pl. 4 (bottom).
Jerusalem, Armenian Patriarchate Library, p. 50.
Kirchner, *Jüdisches Ceremoniel,* Nuremberg, 1734, p. 51 (left).
Formerly Detroit, Charles Feinberg Collection, p. 55 (top left), 83 (top), 97.
Paris, M. Kugel Collection, p. 55 (bottom right).
Photo Alinari, Florence, p. 58.
Cecil Roth Collection, p. 71, 81, 96.
Amsterdam, Rijksmuseum, p. 74.
New York, Jewish Theological Seminary Library, p. 80.
B. Chagall, *Burning Lights,* New York, 1946, p. 86.
New York, Oscar Gruss Collection, p. 92.
Leon J. Obermayer, Philadelphia, Pa., p. 94.
Journal of the American Jewish Historical Society, vol. 40, p. 95.
Photo A. Lewkowicz, Jerusalem, p. 96.
Tel Aviv Museum, p. 99.
Jerusalem, Keren Kayemet le-Israel Photo Archives, p. 100 (left); color: pl. 3 (bottom).
Photo Werner Braun, Jerusalem, p. 103 (bottom); color: pl. 2 (left), 3 (top), 6, 7 (bottom).
Budapest, Museum of Fine Arts, p. 104.
Jerusalem, Ben-Zvi Institute, p. 107.
London, William Margulies Collection, pl. 4 (top).
Photo David Rubinger, Jerusalem, pl. 8.

Cover: "The Masked Ball," engraving after a drawing by P. Wagenaar, 1780. Jerusalem, Israel Museum.